PAT NOLAN

BORN UPON THE TIDE

STORIES OF IRISH MEN OF THE SEA

GW00750635

The
History
Press
Ireland

Front cover image: Landing the catch at Inver Strand. (George Gallagher)
Back cover: *Celtic Explorer* on the high seas.

First published 2017

The History Press Ireland
50 City Quay
Dublin 2
Ireland
www.thehistorypress.ie

The History Press Ireland is a member of Publishing Ireland,
the Irish book publisher's association.

British Library Cataloguing in Publication Data.
A catalogue record for this book is available from the British Library.

ISBN 978 0 7509 8561 1

Typesetting by Geethik Technologies, origination by The History Press
Printed and bound by TJ International

CONTENTS

Introduction   5

1. A Gamut of Seagoing   7
    Jim Moore of Portavogie, County Down

2. Accountancy Not For Peter   21
    Peter Campbell of Skerries, County Dublin

3. One Hundred Years of Service   31
    Paddy Hodgins of Clogherhead, County Louth

4. Carrick-a-Rede Salmon Fishery   41
    Acki Colgan of Ballintoy, County Antrim

5. Steadfast in his Beliefs   50
    Arthur Reynolds of Dún Laoghaire/Bergen

6. Spent a Lifetime Fishing   58
    Seamus Corr of Skerries, County Dublin

7. A Man For All Seasons   73
    George Gallagher of Inver, County Donegal

8. Resolute Beliefs   93
    Brian Crummy of Dún Laoghaire/Dunmore East

9. Born in a Lighthouse   100
    Ted Sweeney of Blacksod/Belmullet, County Mayo

10. Died Just Over a Year Ago   113
    Marion, Andy and John of North Donegal

11. Kerry Blood in their Veins   122
    Pat Moore of Killybegs, County Donegal

12. Wouldn't Change a Thing   132
    Michael O'Driscoll of Schull, County Cork

13. Throw Him Out!   141
    John Francis Brosnan of Dingle, County Kerry

14. Reflections of an Octogenarian   150
    Frank Kiernan of Kinsale, County Cork

Acknowledgements   159

INTRODUCTION

This book was born out of my interest in recording the experiences of men who have been to sea. If left undocumented, such experiences – ways of life really – will quickly fade into oblivion. My motivation is to help keep the memory of such ways of life alive.

Born Upon the Tide reflects the variety of experiences – opinions, memories, humorous incidences and occasional disasters – as recalled by the men I met on my travels around the coastline of Ireland.

While the book focuses on the lives and times of commercial fishermen, there is also substantial space given to men with deep-sea and related shore-work experience. Irrespective of vocation, all the men who have contributed to this book have an intimate knowledge of the sea and the often tough life that goes with it.

1

A GAMUT OF SEAGOING

Jim Moore of Portavogie, County Down

It had been fifty odd years since I last travelled along the splendid scenic coastal route of the Ards Peninsula in County Down. During the course of a recent telephone conversation with Portavogie native, Captain Jim Moore, I gathered that many changes had taken place in the interim. When I asked the good captain if it might be possible to have a chat with him regarding his lifetime experiences, the response was, 'No problem, I will be delighted to meet you, and by the way, Jim is the name.' A date was arranged there and then!

On arrival at Portavogie I drove towards the pier. What I saw before me bore no resemblance to what had existed all those years ago. I spoke to a gentleman out walking a dog and raised the subject of how the pier had changed since I'd last seen it. 'Well,' he said, 'there have been two major develop-ments in that time, one in the 1970s and another in the 1980s. The actual size of the pier has been doubled and a completely new structural arrangement was put in place in order to improve shelter facilities. A slipway has also been incorporated and the basin has been deepened. As you can see, there is also a large marketing hall/area and an ice-making machine. It is very different indeed.' Berthed at the pier, in addition to a number of smaller boats, there were upwards of twenty large trawlers (70–80ft), the vast majority of which were timber-hulled and of Scottish origin.

Jim's bungalow was easy to find and the man himself answered the door and warmly welcomed me to Portavogie. Comfortably seated inside and with the small talk over, Jim began to relate his memories.

I was born on 18 January 1933. My parents were local and my father was a fisherman. While attending the Public Elementary School from the age of 10 years onwards, all boys were gearing up for the only career on offer – fishing! That was it, no other

Jim Moore at his Portavogie home.

career was ever considered. That being so, when I left school in 1947 I went straight into my father's fishing vessel as a crewman. The exact date was 26 July 1947.

We fished for hake off the Isle of Man and landed our catch nightly at Peel. As the year moved on we went into the Clyde and fished out of Campbeltown and Girvan. Coming up to Christmas we moved to Ardglass; a very busy port in those days. Boats and men from the north-east Scottish ports of Peterhead, Fraserburgh, Macduff, Buckie, Hopeman and Lossiemouth came in great numbers. Among them came the men who are reputed to have introduced seine netting to the north of Ireland in 1934 – brothers Willie and Jimmy, members of a famous Thomson fishing family.

In addition to the Scotch boats, you also had the Mourne men coming from Kilkeel and Annalong. Yes, Ardglass was indeed a very busy port in those days. To add to the confusion, it was necessary to land catches by 6pm so that buyers could get their purchases transported in time to catch the Belfast to Heysham Ferry. Whiting was the predominant catch landed; anything else was mere by-catch.

Jim remained in that particular fishing scene for three and a half years. During that time he was in daily contact with men who had returned from having done stints on merchant ships. Men tended to join the Merchant Navy whenever fishing was poor. It was a practice akin to that carried out by migrant workers. After their overseas travels, the men spoke glowingly of the wonderful places they had been to the marvels they had seen, and generally eulogised about the continuous sunshine and blue skies of faraway places. Furthermore, whilst out fishing, whenever a merchant ship passed by, not only were the old hands able to name the ship's owner, they also knew where it was coming from and where it was going to. As time passed, Jim was influenced by what he heard and decided to personally experience life on the high seas.

In January 1951 he joined a Burns & Laird Line (B&L) ferry ship running between Belfast and Glasgow. It was a fairly short-lived job as the ageing ship was broken up a year later. Jim stayed on with the B&L Line for a period of time during which he did relief work. Next he moved on to permanent employment with the Kinsale Head Line, a shipping company that worked out of Belfast and ran ships to Baltic Sea ports. Then aged around 19, Jim has fond memories of those days. He recalls the ship taking on coal at a port on the east coast of Scotland for transportation to Danish destinations such as Korsor and Copenhagen. Having unloaded the coal, the next assignment was to sail further on up the Baltic Sea, occasionally to its extremity, and take on timber at Swedish and Finnish ports for transportation back to Belfast and Dublin. For a moment he reflected before saying, 'To me, Denmark was and still is a wonderful country.'

Not one to stand still, a year or so after joining B&L, Jim moved on to an Ellermen Papayanni Line ship, the 5,000-ton *Maltasian*, engaged in running general cargo, and occasionally full loads of potatoes when in season, to Mediterranean Sea ports. Having discharged the cargo, it was usual to take on oranges and other fruits for shipping back to the UK. However, one trip was to be very different. Before leaving London, orders were received to take on a cargo of timber for the UK at a Black Sea port. The cargo was in fact to be taken on at Constanza, Romania, which was then behind the Iron Curtain. Jim reminded me:

> It was 1954 and the Cold War between the USA and the Soviet Union was at its coolest. There were all sorts of stories told about how foreign sailors who stepped out of line in Soviet-controlled countries were harshly dealt with. Nevertheless, with all its intrigue, uncertainties and dangers the crew were looking forward to the adventure.

Having discharged the last part of its outbound cargo in Salonika, Greece, the *Maltasian* set sail for Constanza, via Istanbul and Zonguldak, a small port on the north coast of Turkey. Jim continued:

> As we approached the Romanian coast, Russia's centuries-old punishment of sending undesirables to Siberia for the most trivial of offences was very much on our minds. No one wanted to spend the remainder of their days in those infamous 'salt mines'. Around 5 p.m. we dropped anchor. Immediately customs and port officials boarded. The crew were mustered and all accommodation was thoroughly searched. A medical examination, including checking for venereal diseases, was carried out by a doctor. The ship was cleared to berth at midnight. We spent the following ten days loading timber – the only western nation ship at the port. Thirty-six hours' notice was required of crew members who wished to go ashore. Intense security and strict regulations were in operation at all times. I recall that we were in Constanza on the day in 1954 when, against the odds, West Germany won the World Cup by defeating the highly fancied and crack Hungarian team of that era by a scoreline of 3-2. Sailing away from the port we had the same number of crew members as when we arrived. Things turned out not to be as bad as they had been painted. It was an experience that will stay with me for the rest of my life; all the memories are still fresh in my mind.

Following what Jim describes as, 'A wonderful time on the beautiful Ellermen Papayanni Line ship', he joined the Canadian Pacific Railway Line, a company that then ran a passenger service from Liverpool to Montreal or, in the wintertime, to Halifax or St John's when the St Lawrence River froze over. The line also ran twenty-day West Indies cruises from New York during the winter months. He went on to say how fortunate he was to have worked on two magnificent ships on those trips. He served as quartermaster on the *Empress of Australia* and as an able seaman (AB) on the *Empress of Scotland*. In those days, going ashore in Cuba was a formality and Havana was, he says, 'A beautiful city'.

While life was good, the years were passing by and Jim had an unfulfilled ambition – he wanted to become an officer. To facilitate that aspiration, he took a relief job in one of the John Kelly (Belfast) ships trading around the British Isles. In that way he had an opportunity to study and, as time went on, to chop and change between shipping companies where he gained the necessary experience to further his cause. Over a period of nine years between 1956 and 1965, he worked for and achieved Certificates of Competency at all levels – Mates Certificate (1956), Masters Home Trade Certificate (1960), 2nd Mates Foreign Going (1962), and the ultimate Masters Foreign Going Certificate (1965). Along the way he married Cissie in 1962.

Having acquired his qualifications, Captain James Moore returned to sea. He went to a Glasgow company, Gem Line, better known as Robertsons of Glasgow. He had previously worked with the Gem Line company during the period of 'experience gaining' for his Masters Foreign Going Certificate of Competency.

However, now he had a young family growing up at home who, on his return from long trips, were beginning to ask their mother, 'Who is that man?' Yes, home life was more or less non-existent! Jim, who was by then 34 years of age, and Cissie sat down to discuss what was best for the future. The conclusion reached was that it would not be right for him to go on spending so much time away from home. But what was he to do between then and retirement age – thirty years hence! Inevitably, a return to fishing came up as an option. The arguments made in favour of fishing pointed towards the fact that good money was being made at the time, he had been a fisherman in the past, many of his mates were fishermen, and he knew everyone involved. Why not give it a go! He would purchase his own boat. Should things not work out for whatever reason, he had the qualifications to go back to sea at any time. Although it was a major step, Jim and Cissie decided to follow their instincts. He retired from the merchant shipping way of life in October 1967.

Five months later, on 23 March 1968, Jim purchased a boat that was at that time fishing out of Ayr. She was named *Kincora*, a 70ft Tyrrell-built Lossiemouth boat, owned by Jimmy Thomson. Quoting Jim, 'I had the *Kincora* for the next fourteen years; it was one of the happiest and prosperous periods of my life.'

By 1982 the *Kincora* had over thirty years of service behind her and was at a stage where she was beginning to need a lot of maintenance. Therefore Jim decided to sell her. A replacement came in the form of the Killybegs-based, Norwegian-built *Sanpaulin*, owned by the legendary fisherman, Tommy Watson. Her stay under Jim's stewardship was relatively short – a couple of years or so – mainly because she had deep draft, which did not suit Portavogie harbour.

The next boat to come under his ownership was the *Mayflower*, a 66ft Lossiemouth vessel, built at the Herd and Mackenzie Yard in 1957. He bought her on 6 June 1984. When it came to re-registering the boat, the date of purchase corresponded with D-Day (6 June 1944) so he used the digits '44', i.e. 'B44'. Jim had a long association with her as she remained in the family for twenty-four years. When he retired as skipper on 11 November 1994, his son Ashley, who now works for the Belfast Harbour Board, took over. By then the boat was getting old and the decision was made to sell her. So ended Jim's direct involvement with fishing, but he is still able to recall how the fishing scene in the north-east port of Portavogie unfolded over a period of many years.

The *Mayflower* with the McCammon Rocks (Portavogie) off the port stern quarter.

When I asked Jim to tell me a little of the changes that had taken place, this is what he had to say:

During the 1930s the main types of fishing here were herring drifting and anchor seining. After the Second World War ring-netting came in, a lot of which was carried out by local boats in the Clyde. Circa 1955 trawling began to emerge as the foremost method of fishing. While it became well established during the 1960s, with prawns being an important part of the catch, a few ringers continued to work out of here. From the early to mid-1970s, influenced by Scotch and Isle of Man fishermen, queen scallop/queenie dredging became significant. From around 1976 onwards there was a decline in demand for queenies, resulting in a drop on prices paid. Consequently some boats returned to trawling. Prawns and whitefish, including whiting, cod, and hake to a lesser extent, became the main catch. For the most part, fishing was virtually non-existent during the month of May – often referred to as 'hungry May': when boats underwent annual overhaul and cleanup. In late May and early June, herring began to show up. While not yet plentiful, prices were good. Towards the end of June or early July, they arrived in copious amounts and continued as such until well into September. As time went on, big boats with powerful engines did really well at the herring. Come October it was back to trawling.

As with all County Down fishing fleets, a great deal of their time was spent harvesting the waters away from home, with the Isle of Man sea area, the Solway Firth, the Galloway coast and Firth of Clyde being most frequented. On a personal level, Jim concentrated a great deal on queenie dredging. He found it to be very profitable fishing. There was, he said:

> Big fishing and for the most part prices were good at around £5 per bag. A normal catch for two days was around 100 bags. We landed at Peel when fishing off the Isle of Man. It was a case of two days at sea, a night in Peel, and back out the next day. When fishing further south and closer to the mainland we occasionally landed to a Scottish merchant at Garston, a port on the Mersey. We also queenie fished in Cardigan Bay. It used to take us fifteen hours from Portavogie harbour to the fishing grounds. We left home on Monday, made two landings at Holyhead, and returned home on Friday. The dredges we used were made in Peel and required quite a bit of maintenance.

As for the development of fishing on the County Down coast, especially the move away from drift netting to seining, Jim believes much is owed to the Scotsmen who came to Ardglass. They were, he said, 'miles ahead of us'. He attributes the progressiveness of the Scots to the fact that their boats tended to be new and were equipped with top-class fishing gear. Those who owned the boats were frequently wealthy professionals and businessmen who had no direct link with fishing, but who had lots of money to invest where it mattered most, in providing the best of boats and gear. It was a major advantage to have an experienced, well-informed and open-minded skipper, who might also be a shareholder. It was also claimed that a famous net-making firm at Elgin, close to Lossiemouth on the Moray Firth, worked very closely with local fishermen, to the extent of putting nets into boats and monitoring effectiveness. As a result of consultation between skipper and net maker, alterations were made to enhance performance. It is said that legendary fisherman Willie Thomson, who went on to become a prolific whiting catcher, and indeed was decorated by King George VI for his expertise, benefited greatly from working in such an environment.

In contrast, boats on the County Down coast were likely to be skipper- and/or family-owned, well-used, second-hand Scotch vessels requiring a great deal of costly maintenance. The financial backing prevalent on the Scottish scene was not readily available in County Down. The tendency was to go on doing what had always been done – the same old fishing methods using traditional gear. As such, local men were dependent on their Scotch counterparts to pioneer the way and share in their experience and expertise. The arrival of the Lossiemouth Thompson brothers, Willie and Jimmy, to fish out of Ardglass in the mid-1930s heralded a new era in fishing on the Irish coast. They were the men who had revolutionised fishing off the north-east coast of Scotland, specialising in seine netting for whiting. Quoting Jim:

> Being the gentlemen they were, they willing supplied information based on their experiences to advance the cause of their County Down colleagues in every way possible. As a result, standards of fish catching and fish handling improved greatly. Neither did they shy away from pointing out to their fellow skippers that if they were to really advance they needed

to invest in bigger, more powerful boats. By the late 1940s around twenty-four boats, many of them Scottish, fished from Portavogie in the wintertime. The use of seine nets ensured that very large landings of whiting were recorded. As time went by and the Thompsons of Lossiemouth moved on to fish the whole Irish coast, the legacy of knowledge on seine net fishing they passed on to local fishermen at many ports left an indelible mark on the development of fishing on this island.

Jim went on to tell me of an earlier Portavogie fishing era. He spoke glowingly of 'a great relationship' that built up between Portavogie fishermen and their Kinsale counterparts before the First World War. It was in an era frequently spoken and written about when mackerel drift netting off the south-west coast of Ireland attracted vessels from far and wide. Apparently the Portavogie men greatly looked forward to the annual southward venture. Jim explained:

The boats left here around St Patrick's Day. All going well they would reach their destination two days later. Occasionally they sheltered in Dún Laoghaire on the way. Once in Kinsale, the boats remained based there until late June when they returned home in time to scrub up and paint for the Twelfth of July celebrations. The fishing grounds stretched westwards from the entrance to Cork harbour to the mouth of the Shannon, with the ports of Baltimore, Valentia [Knightstown] and Fenit further bases for large fleets. Any season a Portavogie crewman earned £25 was considered good; £15 was fair, while £10 was poor. It was not unknown for boats to return home in debt. That's the way it was! Once the First World War started, German U-boats became very active off the south coast and that really was the beginning of the end for the Kinsale mackerel fishing. That the great Cunard liner *Lusitania* had the misfortune to fall victim to a German U-boat torpedo attack

11 miles off the Old Head of Kinsale in May 1915 has been well chronicled. By the time the war ended the market for mackerel had collapsed. The young men who went to Kinsale from Portavogie never forgot it; even to their dying days they talked about it. It was the highlight of their lives – the furthest they had travelled, and a definite purple patch. They talked about how nice the people were and importantly that the girls were more beautiful than any others. Yes, it would appear that even the lights shone brighter in Kinsale than anywhere else! Of course they had plenty of time to socialise as in those days they landed fish on Saturday morning and didn't go back out until Monday night.

As mentioned earlier, the harbour complex at Portavogie bears no resemblance to what I recalled in the early 1960s, so I asked Jim about the transformation that had taken place. His run-down on the developments went back to a time when there wasn't a harbour or pier at Portavogie. Before 1900 no harbour existed: boats lay inside a nearby rocky ridge, known as McCammon Rocks, which offered reasonably good shelter. Catches of fish were rowed ashore in punts and landed at a spot known as Cully or Mahood's Gut. (Cully and Mahood were the main fish buyers at the time.) Work commenced in 1900 on the construction of a harbour at the present-day site. It ran into difficulties around 1906, due to lack of funding. However, the project was completed by 1910. In 1917 additional work was carried out, including the provision of a facility whereby logs could be placed across the inside entrance in adverse weather conditions – an arrangement similar to that at Clogherhead Dock.

By the early 1950s the harbour was no longer fit for purpose, due to the fact that the fleet had grown considerably and safety had become a problem. Redevelopment work began in 1952. For a period of three years, the fleet was obliged to use nearby harbours while work was in progress.

Portavogie Pier, September 2011.

Improvements made, costing £270,000, included structural work and dredging. Further redevelopments in 1975 and 1985 have resulted in the greatly enlarged and highly impressive harbour complex that incorporates a purpose-built dock and fish market hall. Since 1976 boats land catches directly to the market hall rather than on to the quay, as had previously been the case.

My long, informative and interesting chat with Jim was drawing to a close when he invited me to go and view his collection – of what, I wasn't sure at the time, but I expected to see a few model boats. He led the way to the attic, where it turned out that the entire space, floor, walls and ceiling, was chock-a-block with an extraordinarily colourful miscellany of model seagoing vessels of all kinds (many of which were made by Jim), photographs, posters, and multiple items of memorabilia, including football club mementos and a host of other knick-knacks. Many of the bits and pieces had been brought from overseas. To say I was flabbergasted is an understatement. It is a truly amazing collection. What a pity a suitable centre can't be found to publicly display such a fascinating assortment.

What an interesting afternoon I spent at Portavogie with the ever so cordial Captain James Moore!

2

ACCOUNTANCY NOT FOR PETER

Peter Campbell of Skerries, County Dublin

Retired fisherman Peter Campbell is a long-time resident of Skerries. Many years ago he arrived there to visit a friend. During his stay, he met Teddy Ferguson, a local fisherman of high repute. Peter, who was interested in a berth on a fishing boat, made Teddy aware of his availability. In time a crew vacancy arose in the Ferguson family-owned boat, the BIM 50-footer *Ros Cathail*, and Peter got the nod. So began a varied and successful career in the world of commercial fishing.

When I asked where he had resided prior to his arrival in Skerries, Peter replied:

> I was born in Belfast but my parents died when I was young. Because of that I went to live in County Mayo with my aunt. The family had a summer residence on Achill Island where I spent many summers from aged 10 to mid-teens or maybe a

little longer. It was during those years I became friendly with Mick O'Gorman, an islander who later acquired the BIM 56-footer *St Catherine*. The boat, now one of only two BIM 56-footers engaged in fishing, has passed on to his son James. It was with Mick's father that I first started going to sea. I was a helper on his 32ft half-decker engaged in towing basking shark carcasses from the catching grounds in Keem Bay to the processing factory in Purteen harbour. That was my first sea job.

Having completed secondary school education, armed with a Leaving Certificate, Peter spent some time in the world of accountancy. He said, 'It took just six months to find out that that particular route towards lifelong employment was not for me. It was then I discovered Skerries and subsequently began fishing on the Ferguson-owned boat.'

A year down the line he decided to go and do what he had really wanted to do some years previously, i.e. an apprenticeship

Peter Campbell on a summer's day at Skerries.

at Moville. It was the early 1970s and, like most young men of that era with fishing as a livelihood in mind, his target was to get a job on 'a good herring boat'. In those years, he said:

> Mid-watering was the game one wanted to be involved in. I ended up in Georgie Rogan's newly Killybegs-built, 58ft *Golden Sunset*, one of three fishing boats exhibited at the 1971 World Fishing Exhibition at Dún Laoghaire. I gained wide mid-watering experience and made quite a bit of money during my time on the *Golden Sunset*. However, the saying 'all good things come to an end' came into play when, due to fishery closures and scarcity, the herring fishing went into decline – an upsurge followed by a down surge.

By then Peter had reached the ripe old age of 23. What was to be his next move? A Ferguson family-owned boat, the *Ard Gillen*, came up for sale. Determined to carry on with his fishing career, Peter took the bold step of purchasing her. It has to be remembered that he purchased the *Ard Gillen* at a time when many experienced local fishermen couldn't see beyond the 50-footers. That perception was based on very real economic reasoning – larger boats were going to be more expensive to run at a time when the industry as a whole was far from flourishing. How were larger boats engaged in trawling going to generate enough money to make them feasible? Peter is in no doubt that during the 1970s and possibly the early 1980s, 65ft whitefish boats trawling out of Skerries couldn't pay their way. However, if progress was to be made where trawling was concerned, then efficient 'small big boats', i.e. boats larger than 50-footers but smaller than 65- or 70-footers, were seen as the way forward. The 56-footers fitted the bill. They raised the trawling potential of boats a notch by not being overly expensive to operate and at the same time capable of catching huge amounts of fish. Peter said, 'It took time, but the upsurge in modern trawling initiated by the 56-footers in the 1970s gradually gained momentum over the years. It led to incremental increases in timber boat size, and eventually to the modern steel-hulled trawlers of today.'

Peter began fishing the *Ard Gillen* off the east coast. 'We had,' he said, 'some great landings of cod in those early years; we recorded hauls of over one hundred boxes.' In 1980 he moved to the west coast, where, along with John F. Lynch's 52ft, Norwegian-built *Marita*, he pair-trawled in Galway Bay during springtime months. That same year, the *Ard Gillen*, along with a group of six or so other boats, some locals and some visitors, broke new ground by delving into the world of prawn trawling off the west coast for the first time. He recalled that:

Aran Island boats, Kieran Gill's *Ard Scia* and Gregory Conneely's *Connacht Ranger*, both BIM 56-footers, were involved. Because of their size the 56-footers were economically suitable for prawn fishing. Those of us who had experienced prawn fishing on the east coast led the pack. Local knowledge provided by men such as Kieran and Gregory was invaluable. It was a case of both factions liaising closely. That's when commercial prawn fishing off Galway began! The first year, in a matter of a few months, there were £56,000 pounds' worth landed. I predicted that figure would hit the £1 million very quickly and a few years later it did. In those years through pair trawling and working with doors, we also recorded great landings of whitefish. Commonplace was hauls of 200 boxes of mixed whitefish when pairing. Also during door fishing Gregory's *Ard Chluain* caught huge amounts of fish. In pair-fishing the bulk of the catch was made up of whiting. The frequency of poor market prices for that particular species often made fishing them financially uneconomical. In order to overcome the problem, one particular season, I decided to break up the partnership arrangement and take up single-boat trawling. In that way, I was able to target better-quality fish and, at the same time, fish for whiting when the market was good.

When we started trawling inshore off Galway hauls made on new-found pieces of ground still stick in my mind. A three-hour tow on one occasion yielded eleven boxes of monk, ten boxes of megrims, a box of jumbo prawns and three boxes of mixed other fish. It was bordering on phenomenal when you think about it – nearly half a ton of monk, hard to understand it now. For a day's trawling we occasionally landed up to 200 boxes of fish. It was indeed something else.

Peter went on to outline the establishment of Rossaveal as a significant fishing port on the Irish coast. This is what he had to say:

Originally Galway City harbour acted as the principal west-coast fishing port. It was there that the bulk of catches were landed. Following the global oil crisis in 1979, and the result-ant increases in fuel costs, fishermen found that steaming to and from the fishing grounds to Galway harbour became a serious profit-stripping factor. Taking the initiative, Galway and Aran Fishermen's Co-operative commissioned a study aimed at identifying potential sites for the development of appropriate landing facilities closer to the fishing grounds. While Rossaveal fulfilled the criteria set down, the State initially opposed the venture on the basis of the very con-siderable cost involved. However, in the face of widespread pressure, 'the powers that be' capitulated, and in 1981 con-sented to the relocation of the National Fishery Harbour Centre from Galway to Rossaveal.

With the development of the prawn fishery and the establish-ment of Rossaveal as a National Fishery Harbour, the Galway and Aran Fishermen's Co-operative established an auction hall – the first meaningful open auction facility for prawns in Ireland, according to Peter. Local men employed by French companies acted as agents and bid on their behalf. The auction influenced prices considerably and overall proved to be a great success. While demand for whole prawns was beginning to increase, it was still mainly tails that were sought after in the early days of the auction.

In 1983, Peter decided to sell the *Ard Gillen* and raise the profile of his fishing career another notch by investing in a bigger boat. She would be used initially for the development of deep-water prawn and whitefish trawling off the west coast. The boat in question was the transom stern, 82ft *Iuda Naofa* (SO679), built at Mevagh in 1978.

This is how Peter recalls the situation at the time:

> Prior to 1985 there was no conscious effort for Irish boats to fish deep water. It wasn't until around 1984 that the Porcupine Basin was first visited. Coincidentally, or otherwise, it seems that Spanish markets for monkfish, hake and prawns began to open up. Fishermen's co-operatives and processing businesses at a number of locations on the Irish coast became involved. Fleets began to build up, with Castletownbere and Killybegs prominent. As the 1980s progressed, boats hailing from south and east ports, including Skerries, fished the Porcupine Banks, and deepwater trawling off west coast side by side with the Spanish fleet became the norm. With a fleet of good boats now built up a lot of that fishing was done west of Achill and down off the Blasket Islands.

From the early days of herring mid-watering on the *Golden Sunset* to owning and skippering the *Ard Gillen* and *Iuda Naofa*, Peter had spent around twenty years of his life at the coalface of fishing, frequently, along with others, in a pioneering role within the industry.

Tailing pawns on the *Iuda Naofa* off Galway in the 1980s are Pat Byrne and Mel White.

Sometime in the early to mid-1990s, an opportunity in another aspect of fishing presented itself and led to him selling the *Iuda Naofa*. He moved into the mussel business:

> I got involved in the mussel business with a man named Alex McCarthy. As with modern trawling, again I was in at the infancy of the modern upsurge in the mussel business. It was a business traditionally carried on out of Wexford. By setting up a business based in Carlingford Lough we became the first company to break the mould. Up to then there were about eight companies based in and around Wexford; I believe we became the ninth company in Ireland. Now there are about thirty! Once we were successful others followed.

Company vessels used in the Carlingford Lough mussel business and skippered by Peter were the 60ft *Atlantis Belle* (N80) and the 110ft *Cornelis Gerrit* (D669). Of the *Cornelis Gerrit*, he says, 'She was highly successful and her delivery back to Holland in April 2011, where she originally came from,

marked my retirement from sea going.' Owing to the success
of the *Cornelis Gerrit*, the company invested in what might be
described as a super mussel dredger in the form of the 145ft
Wings of the Morning, a vessel more similar in appearance to
today's pelagic trawlers than to the old traditional dredger.

When I asked Peter for one highlight from his fishing career,
he thought for a moment and, to my surprise, chose his involvement with the Irish Fishermen's Organisation (IFO). The fact
that there were representatives from virtually every harbour
on the coast and that he got to know individuals from all over
was something he really enjoyed. Working in conjunction with
people such as Joey Murrin and Mick Orpen was interesting,
to say the least. He also recalled serving as vice-chairman with
the legendary Joe Maddock in the chair. Overall, he said, 'There
were good times and bad. The bad times were harbour block-
ades fronted by the IFO, fuel crises, herring fishery closures and
the sometimes stormy relations with our European friends. The
herring fishery difficulties that led to some members spending
time in prison was probably the worst time.'

Peter on the *Iuda Naofa* in the 1980s.

One particular incident during his fishing career that brought a smile to Peter's face was that of a 'citizen's arrest' on the 'high seas'. Looking back, the incident seems somewhat amusing but it probably wasn't so at the time. It occurred in his early years fishing off the west coast, when a number of Irish boats, including the *Ard Gillen*, arrested a French trawler that had towed through and damaged the nets of a local boat. Having surrounded the vessel and escorted it to Rossaveal, through the services of the fluent French-speaking Co-operative sub-manager, an amicable arrangement was arrived at: the crew of the offending vessel undertook to mend and fully restore the damaged net. With the job satisfactorily completed on Rossaveal Pier, the French vessel was allowed to go on its way. A nice wee story!

As I bade Peter farewell, he sat contentedly with his daughter, enjoying the brilliant afternoon sunshine on Skerries seafront. The fully occupied seats and tables that lined the

Cornelis Gerrit (D669).

pavement outside Joe May's and the other brightly coloured seafood bar restaurants gave that particular part of the north County Dublin resort a distinctive continental ambience. Yes, it's easy to see why Skerries, with its attractive seafront, is one of Dublin's most desirable residential and holiday destinations.

My own visit to Skerries was made all the more enjoyable by the encounter with the retired, highly experienced fisherman, the *almost* youthful-looking Peter.

3

ONE HUNDRED YEARS OF SERVICE

Paddy Hodgins of Clogherhead, County Louth

I welcomed the opportunity to call on Paddy Hodgins, a renowned Clogherhead man. The now 87-year-old hale and hearty gentleman, who has spent the greater part of his life-time associated with the commercial fishing scene at the port, was happy to meet me. 'No problem,' he said. 'Come along to my home on the Harbour Road, adjacent to Port Oriel.'

Before going inside the house, Paddy drew my attention to the striking and uninterrupted views of the Cooley and Mourne Mountains to the north, while to the distant south lay the unmistakable mass of Lambay Island. Sandwiched between and extending over a distance of 40 or 50 miles is a stretch of the Irish Sea. While there are times when it can be an extremely turbulent body of water, on that day it was a shimmering plane.

Paddy on Clogherhead Pier.

I was greatly looking forward to hearing of Paddy's varied seafaring experiences. The extremely fresh-looking octogenarian began his story:

My family have had one hundred years of service at the harbour. Starting with my grandfather, just after the old pier was built in the 1880s, he was the second harbour master to be appointed there. He held the post until 1919, when my father replaced him. On his retirement in 1950, I took over and remained in the post until 1996. I believe it's fair to say that we kindly but firmly cared for the comings and goings of fishing vessels and their crews. When I first took over, things were simple enough, part-time really, but it developed as time went on and became virtually a 24/7 job; a full-time way of life! Duties included seeing to pier lighting, regulating berths, collecting fees and making sure that boats using the harbour were accounted for.

With reference to keeping an eye on craft activity at sea, he deemed the location of his residence as prime:

> I had a great view of the bay, north and south. The boats' comings and goings were readily visible. Then when the radio telephone came into being you could listen to what was happening and you'd know that everyone was safe. I always got on well with those who used the harbour. I came across great characters down through the years. Surnames synonymous with fishing in Clogherhead abound! For generations there have been very well-known and respected families such as the Kirwans, Sharkeys, Tallons, Connollys, and then you also had the Burkes and Farrells. Current members of those families are still fishing and, like their forbearers, are great fishermen.

Paddy is recognised far and wide as one of life's gentlemen and needs no introduction to the majority of Irish fishermen, north or south. Not only was he harbour master at Clogherhead, but he was also a part-time BIM agent there for thirty years. In fact, it has been said that if you answer 'yes' to the question, 'Have you ever been to Clogherhead?', the next question will be, 'Did you meet Paddy Hodgins?' Further reinforcement of that belief comes in Warren Nelson's foreword to Paddy's book, *Clogherhead – Through My Eyes*, where he states, 'Paddy Hodgins as boy, young man, fisherman, lifeboat man and harbour master *is* Clogherhead for many people, either local or the stream of visitors from all parts.' Paddy was, and still is, proactive in furthering causes beneficial to the local community.

He recalls becoming a crew member of Bernard Sharkey's *Gola* at the age of 15 in 1945. The 54ft *Gola*, powered by a 50hp Skandia engine, was, by the standards of the time, a substantial, well-maintained and well-equipped fishing vessel. He spent three seasons herring-drifting out of Howth and the Isle of Man. Isle of Man catches were mostly landed in Ardglass. 'It was,' he said, 'a great treat to go into Ardglass, where you could purchase white bread, tea, sugar, bags of coal and oil – "luxuries" unattainable south of the border in those early post-war years.' From those days he also recalls first meeting a Kilkeel teenager, Gerry Doyle. They became pals to the extent that Gerry gave Paddy the odd bucket of coal to keep the stove of the *Gola* burning. It was a time when fuel shortage in the south of Ireland was such that Paddy was reduced to using chunks of old rope to heat up the *Gola*'s stove.

Since the greater part of his working life, and indeed that of his father and grandfather, took place in and around the harbour, he has an in-depth knowledge of happenings there. One thing that quickly became clear is that down through the centuries and until recent times those who fished from the port did so in harbour conditions that were scarcely fit for purpose. Inadequate landing facilities and grossly unsafe berthing places left men at their wits' end as to how to make a living and, at the same time, prevent their vessels being wrecked whenever storms blew up. It wasn't until the 1800s that attempts were made by the powers that be to improve the situation, albeit meagre attempts. Developments in the late 1820s included the excavation of an inner harbour, variously referred to as the 'Inner Dock', the 'Dock', and the 'Old Dock'. It incorporated a single, narrow entrance and a stone-built slipway at the far end. It was tidal and did little to improve the situation since seas rolling through the entrance during winter gales caused significant wave turbulence within the otherwise enclosed space. As a result, conditions in the 'Dock' put boats at risk of being smashed. Fishermen were left with no alternative during bad weather but to haul their yawls out of the water.

In later years, a couple of 42ft luggers, one of them, *The Foundling*, owned by Paddy's grandfather, fished from the port. Because those boats were too big to haul out of the water during winter months, the rather drastic measure of submerging them inside the 'Dock' was normal practice.

Some minor improvements were carried out on the dock in the late 1830s. However, it wasn't until 1927 that significant work was undertaken: the dock was enlarged and facilities for the placement of portable booms were fitted at the narrow entrance. The booms were sturdy 30ft baulks of timber that could be lowered horizontally into guides, one on top of the other, across the entrance, so as to prevent rough sea conditions from extending into the dock. The booms formed a substantial barrier. Boats inside the dock were now safe, regardless of conditions outside.

As harbour master, Paddy was familiar with lowering and lifting the booms. It was an operation, he said, 'that was carried out using a hand-operated crane until it became power-driven in 1964. A tricky job, often urgent, and requiring the assistance of other men. In bad weather it wasn't easy.' While the boomed dock did alleviate some worries regarding the safe berthing of boats, it didn't tick all the boxes. Nevertheless for a period of several decades, boat owners slept more soundly in their beds on stormy nights in the knowledge that an oasis of calm existed. A disadvantage to sheltering in the often-crowded dock was that the waters were tidal. Entering and leaving the dock was restricted to a couple of hours before and after high tide. From the 1990s onwards, significant increases in boat dimensions made the dock virtually redundant. For that reason too the usefulness of the pier was greatly diminished. The owners and skippers of local boats looked elsewhere to land their fish and safely berth their boats.

Where the outer harbour was concerned, no significant attempt at improvement was made until 1885. Even then, the work carried out, which entailed the building of a pier at Port Oriel, fell well short of expectations. The 250ft wall-like structure jutting out into the Irish Sea has been locally described as 'an excuse for a pier'. Not only was it inadequate for its purpose but it also deteriorated badly over the years. Paddy states that, 'While it served fishermen well enough to a certain extent it was never a safe haven; there was too much exposure to the winds.'

It wasn't until the mid-1900s that a concerted effort was made to have that old pier replaced:

> We formed a development association in the 1950s but had to endure a long and tortuous campaign to get to the point where the present splendid pier became a reality. Government ministers of the 1950s/'60s, in the form of Oliver Flannagan and Paddy Donnegan, were sympathetic to the cause, but money was not available for the project. Then in the 1980s when the old pier got an awful hammering during heavy gales, efforts were renewed to get something done. In the first instance a deputation of whom I was a member went to Leinster House and we met with all the relevant bigwigs, including Charles Haughey. We said our piece but again the 'no money' scenario was trotted out. However, we continued to highlight our cause and with the Fishermen's Association growing in strength, politicians were encouraged to visit the port and witness the situation first-hand. Of significance also was the fact that a local councillor, the late John Kirk, took a particular interest in our fight. Eventually, through the efforts of all concerned, we began to see light at the end of the tunnel.

Around 2000, a conglomeration of bodies combined to provide funding for the establishment of an auction hall, an ice plant, workshop units, public toilets and showers. Yet, the actual pier at Port Oriel remained woefully inadequate in many ways. As already stated, local skippers and owners of the large, modern and massively expensive vessels had to look elsewhere for safe berthing places, and also to land their catches.

Dock entrance and exit with Barry Faulkner's *Celtic Cross* (DA10) in the
background.

'Good things come to those who wait' is a phrase extolling
the virtue of patience. That may well be the case where the
fishing fraternity of Clogherhead is concerned because after
all the years of anguish and waiting, slowly but surely, a state-
of-the-art pier was built and finally completed at Port Oriel in
2007. Happily, the present Clogherhead fleet, totalling around
thirty of the finest vessels fishing on the Irish coast, are now
able to berth and land at their home port if they choose to do
so. Fishermen can, for the first time in the history of the port,
leave their boats in the knowledge that the new 'dog leg' pier,
a project that involved a total investment of more than €11
million is a safe haven.

When I asked Paddy what his thoughts were on the changes
he had observed at the port over the years, this is what he had
to say:

From the smallest punt right up to the latest modern trawlers, Clogherhead has always been a place of boats, and every visitor will have carried away with them memories of boats. I've seen a lot of changes in the type of boats working out of here. At first it was yawls – they were propelled by oars and sail. There were twenty-eight of them with five men in each boat. They fished herring in Dundalk Bay and down as far as Balbriggan; then came luggers, sailing vessels of around 40ft in length. In the 1920s, the first motor trawlers arrived. Clogherhead became a great centre for fishing herring, whiting, cod, plaice and ray. Then of course there were the ringers, seine netters, trawlers, and finally the big modern steel boats of today. The arrival of the BIM 50-footers in the late 1950s and early '60s were a tremendous boost to the fleet and to fishing at Clogherhead. In the 1970s, a fish-processing plant, Red Sail, was established by the highly respected Younger family at Port Oriel. It gave employment to 130 people in its heyday and was a great success up to its closure in 2002. Over the years it had helped in no small way to build up the fleet. As far as I can remember, the number of trawlers increased from around five to thirty-three. As well as the local boats, others came from Arklow, Skerries and Balbriggan to fish for prawns off the 'Head' … Prawn fishing started here in 1949. It was one Capt. J.P. Cunningham, a World War II veteran, and an interesting character, locally well known as 'Captain Pat', who first fished for them. Some Kilkeel men may dispute that but I know it to be correct. While serving on Daunt Rock Lightship around that time, Capt. Pat purchased a 45ft boat named the *Radiant Morn* which he fished together with his brother Thomas and other crew.

In relation to prawn fishing at Clogherhead over the years, Paddy had this to say:

I saw it all happening; it became really big. At first the boats got around a £1 a box. For 'tailing' and gut-removing, people

ashore were paid one shilling and six pence per box; that later
rose to two shillings and sixpence. There was always a market
for prawns here. In the early days, Pat Lynch, a local man, did
a tremendous job in finding outlets and as a result he kept
the fleet going. As time went on, processing factories opened
in Kilkeel and Portavogie, providing additional outlets. Whole
prawns were also exported to France and Spain.

Paddy has fond memories of herring-fishing seasons at
Clogherhead too. He recalls Portavogie boats joining the local
drift-netting boats and in later years moving on to 'ringing'
and seining. He also recalls boatloads of whitefish, whiting in
particular, being landed. There were times when prices paid
were so poor that the monetary return didn't cover the transport cost to the Dublin market.

Since the mid-1940s, Paddy has been involved with the
lifeboat service at Clogherhead. He recalls, 'Luke Sharkey and
I are the last surviving crew members of the *Mary Ann Blunt*,
an RNLI vessel first stationed at Clogherhead in 1934.' He
went on to say, 'I also served as Deputy Launching Authority
and Honorary Secretary for many years. To this day I take
a great interest in the service.' Paddy's long years of service
to the institution were recognised at presentations made at
the highly esteemed venues of Áras an Uachtaráin, and the
Barbican Hall, London. Also, his long years of service at the
harbour did not go unnoticed. When Paddy called it a day,
the Fishermen's Association handsomely recognised his years
of valued and unstinting service.

Located adjacent to the church of St Michael, Clogherhead,
is a newly erected Garden of Remembrance to 'Those Lost at
Sea'. Paddy played a major part in the association responsible
for bringing the project to fruition. The striking centre-
piece is a large granite wall plaque listing fifty-five people
under the headings: 'Name', 'Age', 'Area lost', 'Ship', 'Date'.
Elsewhere in the garden, I noticed a smaller granite plaque

with inscriptions on either side of a central divider. On the left: 'Albert D.J. Cashier CO. G. 95th Illinois Infantry US Civil War Fought 1862–1875.' On the right: 'Born Jennie Hodgers Clogherhead 1843–1915.' The person in question was Paddy's late grand-aunt Jennie (the surname Hodgers was changed to Hodgins by his grandmother), who left home unable to read or write, and whose whereabouts were unknown for many years. Disguised as a man, Albert D.J. Cashier, she fought in the US Civil War and retired with an army pension. Not quite your everyday story!

Before leaving Clogherhead, I dropped into the Fisherman's Catch, a very impressive fish shop run by John and Michelle Kirwan; and how could it be other than impressive! Not only are the Kirwan credentials top-drawer where fish and fishing are concerned, but, Jonathan, son of John and Michelle, who skippers the family-owned 24m fishing trawler, *Argonaut IV* (DA22), ensures a supply of top-quality fish to the shop.

On the way to and from the pier, an eye-catching stone-built grotto overlooks the harbour. I stopped to read the inscription. Beneath the over-arching caption, 'Queen of the Sea', the inscription reads, 'In memory of all sailors and fishermen from the area who lost their lives at sea'. Erected by a Luke Sharkey-led Clogherhead Fishermen's Association, it serves as a constant reminder of those who did not return,

'A delight' is the term I would use to describe my visit to Clogherhead. With Paddy kindly acting as 'chauffeur', we visited all the pertinent local sites.

On a sad note, I have to add that Paddy's wife, Joan, the most kindly lady imaginable, has passed away since my visit. May she rest in peace.

4

CARRICK-A-REDE SALMON FISHERY

Acki Colgan of Ballintoy, County Antrim

Located on the North Antrim Coast Road, between Ballycastle and Ballintoy, is Carrick-a-Rede Rope Bridge. It's currently one of Northern Ireland's foremost tourist attractions. Visitors from around the world are exhilarated by the experience of crossing a 100ft chasm on the swaying suspension structure. The bridge, which links tiny Carrick Island to the mainland, has taken many forms over the years. As recently as the 1970s it featured only a single handrail, with large gaps between the foot slats. The current wire-rope and Douglas fir structure is much more substantial. However, what is now sometimes forgotten is that the bridge, which acts as a magnet for hundreds of thousands of visitors annually, owes its origin to local fishermen of the eighteenth century, when it was first put in place to facilitate foot passage to the Carrick-a-Rede Salmon Fishery.

In order to delve into the story of the fishery, I called on Acki Colgan at his Ballintoy home. Acki, now retired, was associated with the fishery throughout his lifetime – right up to its closure in 2002. As boy and man, an indelible link was forged with the fishery through his uncle, who fished there from the 1930s through to the 1970s. Around 1972, Acki took over the reins and continued to fish at Carrick-a-Rede until the fishery finally closed.

First reports of salmon fishing at Carrick-a-Rede and nearby Larrybane date back to 1620. There were several similar fisheries along the North Antrim coast at that time, the most well-known of which were located at Torr Head, Portbraddan and Dunseverick.

Salmon caught at Carrick-a-Rede swam from east to west, close to the north Antrim shoreline, on their way to spawn in the River Bann and the River Bush. So far in did the fish come that they swam into a V-shaped inlet, the apex of which

Acki Colgan at his Ballintoy home.

lay where the mainland and one end of Carrick Island almost converged. The inlet become known as Carrick-a-Rede Salmon Fishery. Lying in wait, with a net at the ready, to greet the salmon, were the fishermen. From the 1600s to around 1840, draft nets were used to entrap the mercurial creatures. There was no intentional meshing involved. In subsequent years, a more efficient catcher known as a 'bag net' was brought in from Scotland.

Draft netting is normally a fairly straightforward operation involving a net being shot in a semi-circular fashion. When fish swim into the net, the circle is completed. The fish are trapped. However, Acki pointed out that it was a difficult and tricky operation to carry out at Carrick-a-Rede:

> The net was shot out from a point on the inside end of Carrick Island and a person high up on the cliff-side kept a lookout for approaching fish. Closing the circle [pulling the net around] would be difficult because the net was particularly deep, nearly

Carrick-a-Rede Rope Bridge, County Antrim, *c.* 1890. (Courtesy of the National Library of Ireland)

10 fathoms of water. At times the strength of the tides caused considerable problems, and the steep rugged hillside running down to the water's edge made for a minimal and tricky standing area on shore.

As I listened to Acki, I soon became aware that a novice lacking expertise needn't bother trying to fish salmon at Carrick-a Rede. If you didn't know exactly where to set the net outwards from, or if you didn't know how to deal with confused tides, and when to expect a 'good run' of fish, or not, as the case may be, then you were not going to make a living salmon-fishing at Carrick-a-Rede. There were multiple factors to be considered. The 'bag net' procedure (draft net replacement), by which fish became entrapped, made for very interesting listening indeed. For yours truly, all was not immediately clear. If it wasn't for the fact that Acki is a patient and pleasant man, he would surely have told me to clear off and stop asking stupid questions. Let's see if I can explain at least some of what was involved. The net was large and heavy – 70 yards long in its entirety. It comprised a 'leader' and a bag portion, with two traps (chambers) totalling 20 yards in length. The 50-yard 'leader' – a net of 3-inch mesh, was suspended vertically in the water by a floating cork-rope. The bag portion, also a netting structure, was three-dimensional when set up for fishing. With the 'leader' fixed to a specific point on the island, the net was shot from a boat and fixed in a precise position, just south of an easterly direction – towards Kenbane Head. The 'old men' regarded those details as vital when setting up the net.

With the net in place, along came the salmon in search of those nearby rivers, but instead they found themselves confronted by the 'leader'. In an attempt to continue on their journey, the fish swam along the 'leader' and were guided into the first of the two traps. Moving on through the smaller entrance (a 6-inch aperture) to the second trap, the fish passed into the final portion of the net (the fish court), from which there was no escape. Typically they would swim round the 'court' by following the path of the net and so would miss the small 6-inch opening in the angled wings of the fish court.

Next it was the business of the boat crew, three or four men, to hand-haul the net and land its content in the boat. That particular job, performed where the sea was nearly 10 fathoms deep, was hard work, when one considers that in 'the good old days' there could be a catch of up to 200 fish to be dealt with. It was for neither weaklings nor the faint-hearted, even when the sea state was moderate. A crew of four was needed and a fairly substantial boat/yawl, considering the 'leader' was 224 3-inch half meshes in depth.

While returns at Carrick-a-Rede Fishery were good for many years, it was a difficult place to fish. As Acki stated, 'Carrick-a-Rede was the most difficult and laborious fishery to work because everything had to be brought on to the island via the bridge and everything, including fish caught, had to be brought back over the bridge.' Obviously, there was lots of heavy and awkward work involved. A major drawback was that all requirements in the way of gear, etc., had to be transported from the mainland across what was an extremely precarious and unsteady rope bridge. It was the fishermen themselves who erected the bridge, which remained until the late 1990s, by which time they had been using it for almost 250 years without mishap.

However, successfully transporting gear onto the island was by no means an end to the difficulties involved for the fishermen. Once the gear was there, it had to be carefully manoeuvred down a steep cliff to a sort of base camp (the fishermen's cottage) about halfway down. From there everything had to be lowered to a boat at sea level by a hand-winch system. The reverse operation had to be undertaken in order to remove items from sea level, which, particularly in the olden days, included lifting the boat from the water on a daily basis. To facilitate the boat-lifting operation, the crew had to attach the boat to a rope rig before getting themselves ashore and commencing winching. Getting on to the shore was very tricky and dangerous when the sea was rough. Often, with 'a bad run coming in', they had to wait and choose a time when conditions were favourable before jumping onto the shore.

Once ashore, the catch had to be taken up the almost vertical rocky hillside and then across that 'shaky bridge' to the mainland. After that, a further rock climb had to be undertaken in order to get to the fish transporter. Acki explained what happened next:

> In the old days whenever there was a lot of fish a local man named McHenry came with a horse and cart and delivered the fish to a nearby ice-house, where it remained overnight. The following morning it was taken by the same mode of transport to Ballycastle railway station and put on the train. The fish was then on its way to market at Manchester. In later years, when Stanley Jamison took over the role of local fish carrier, the horse and cart was replaced by a tractor.

Acki's uncle began fishing at Carrick-a-Rede in 1932. That fishery, like all others on the north Antrim coast at the time, was property of a landed-gentry family – a British social class, consisting of landowners who could live entirely off rental income. Carrick-a-Rede fishery was in the ownership of the Fullerton Estate. As Acki put it:

> My uncle simply fished for a wage paid to him by the Fullerton Estate. All fish caught were property of the estate, the collecting and marketing of which was the business of the estate's Ballycastle-based agent. There was a pile of salmon caught at Carrick-a-Rede over the years, on occasions up to 400 or 500 per day. The bumper year was 1962. That was the best year my uncle fished there. From then on it was really downhill.

During the late 1960s, the Fullerton Estate decided to offload Carrick-a-Rede Fishery. The numbers of fish landed per season were in decline. A drop in revenue was probably the main reason for the sale. As the fishery is situated in an area of outstanding natural beauty, unsurprisingly, The National Trust – Northern Ireland acquired ownership. The intention of the Trust was to lease or rent out the fishery. The local fishermen who undertook the arduous task of annually erecting and taking down the bridge – those familiar with the whole Carrick-a-Rede Fishery scene – were the only possible clients. Acki's uncle and another local man, Pat Donnelly, became The National Trust tenants. They were keen that Acki should join them, but he said:

> By then fishing at Carrick-a-Rede was in decline. The number of salmon being caught was dropping off year by year. My family were young and I had a good enough job. Sean Morton, Ballycastle, then decided to go along with them. In the early 1970s, my uncle, then an old man with failing health, was forced into retirement. Indeed, he passed away shortly afterwards. It was at that point Pat and Sean coaxed me to go in with them – that's how I became seriously involved and remained so through thick and thin over the following thirty years. I remained until 2002, when the Fishery finally closed. I should add that where the operation was concerned, going into the Fishery was no big deal for me as over the years while otherwise employed I always kept in close touch with what went on at the Fishery.

With catch sizes no longer being what they were, I asked Acki if it was possible to make a living from the returns:

> Well, if you had a good season it was alright, but if you had a poor season, then other employment had to be found in winter time. You nearly always needed another source of income; there was no fortune to be made. Perhaps it was always the

same, even to some extent in my uncle's time; it was something you were hooked on. The older men would leave secure jobs and 'go to the salmon'. It has to be remembered that the season was short anyway. At one time, in my uncle's early days, there used to be 'a run' of salmon around the end of March but that died out completely. Following that, fish didn't show up until around the end of May, with a gradual build-up in numbers until a peak was reached, spanning a period over the last week of June and first week of July. Good fishing used to continue until around the end of July. But the overall decline was always in evidence – the numbers of fish caught per season was dropping off alarmingly. Funny thing about salmon, we had a fairly good year in 1989. A lot depended on weather conditions. In Carrick-a-Rede we looked for a good breeze of north-west wind. If the wind went east you might as well go home. It got to be that there was really only three weeks in the season, and if the conditions were not favourable you were in trouble. When, years ago, there was 'a decent piece of fishing' up to the peak of the season, you could have covered your expenses before the peak. In later years that didn't happen, you had to depend on the 'run of fish' at the peak to cover everything. It was always said that if you hadn't your season made before 12 July the outlook wasn't good. For a number of years when there was a few fish going we were able to keep a crew but it got to be in the finish that everybody lost interest; there were days when you waited in vain for help to turn up. The last year we landed a total of 250 salmon for the season. That wouldn't pay anyone!

When I enquired as to why the salmon, which at one time had been so plentiful, had virtually disappeared off the scene, Acki replied:

Too much pressure on them, over fished! The fish had been getting smaller. It stands to reason. For hundreds, thousands of

years, only a minimal amount of salmon had been ta
the sea. Then, over a span of seventy years or less, partic.
during the 1960s and early 1970s when every craft on ti.
coast capable of floating had a train of salmon nets, massive
amounts of fish were removed. They were cleaned out! Blame
for the decline was levelled in individual directions but the
huge overkill has to be shouldered by all, should they be net, or
rod-and-line men.

My afternoon with Acki had passed by all too quickly. It was a
Friday and smiling grandchildren were calling to visit Granda.
However, I squeezed in one further question about the nets
used, to which Acki replied:

> They were very deep and heavy to lift. In the old days, nets
> were knit during the winter, mounted on ropes and made ready
> for fishing – a lot of work – they were paid a few pounds for
> their trouble. Material first used was hemp. That was followed
> by cotton. Hemp nets were heavier and probably stronger than
> cotton. Both types had a lifetime of just three years. Nylon nets
> first came to Carrick-a-Rede in the 1960s. The first net was
> too light and wrapped itself around the corks, etc. The last net
> was made of heavier black nylon. Provided a shark or the likes
> didn't get entangled in them, they would last indefinitely.

Although this fishery was virtually on my doorstep, I knew
very little about it until my so informative visit to Acki.

A piece of information for any strangers intending to visit
the great man at Ballintoy – Acki, was actually christened
Alexander. However, it would be pointless to enquire after
Alexander Colgan; nobody of that name lives there, you will
be told. He is universally known by his nickname – though
nobody, including himself, seems to know the origin of the
rather unusual moniker.

5

STEADFAST IN HIS BELIEFS

Arthur Reynolds of Dún Laoghaire/Bergen

A few years ago, when I received a letter from the maritime stalwart Arthur Reynolds, founder of *The Irish Skipper*, I believe my research into aspects of Irish commercial fishing received a creditable boost. The opening lines of the letter, penned by the man who went on to edit *The Irish Skipper* for twenty-seven years (1964–91), read as follows, 'I have watched with great interest your writings on our fishing vessels and consider your studies to be of great value to future maritime historians.' His letter also included an invitation to meet up and have a chat at a time when he was not in Bergen, where he and his wife, Broghild, reside for much of the year. Our meeting did come to pass on an August afternoon at his Dún Laoghaire apart-ment. Arthur was all that I expected: highly intelligent, widely knowledgeable, experienced in many aspects of life, deeply interested in furthering the Irish fishing industry, steadfast in his beliefs, and a real gentleman.

Although our discussion was wide and varied, the Irish fishing industry took pride of place. As always, it's best to start at the beginning. Arthur was born in Dublin in 1930, the son of an electrician who was involved in the cinema business, and who also had a small transformer-manufacturing plant. The young Arthur was educated at St Patrick's Cathedral Grammar School, Dublin, where one teacher in particular significantly influenced his future thinking and outlook on life in general. That teacher was none other than John de Courcy Ireland, Irish maritime historian, radical politician, humanist, teacher, linguist, founder member of CND in Ireland, and recipient of worldwide honours. Significantly, he has been described as, 'a true friend of seafarers'.

John de Courcy Ireland's considerable involvement with the Labour Party that undoubtedly led to Arthur becoming an active member at the age of 17. By then, his secondary school education was reaching completion and soon the bright young

Arthur Reynolds at his Dún Laoghaire residence.

academic, aided by the odd scholarship or two, was to spend
time at third-level academical institutions in Dublin and Paris.
In Dublin he attended the National College of Art, which was
linked to Trinity College. As for his time in 'Gay Paree' as a
student at the French state art school, well, let's just say that
fun was had. Eventually he decided that enough was enough
and abandoned the delights of Paris in favour of employment
in London – a career in journalism. As he put it, 'I became a
journalist because I was good at writing in school.'

He returned to Dublin and in time sought out a mission
that he believed in and could advance through his input. He
found such a mission, albeit by chance:

> I was always a boating person and wrote a casual article about
> a trawling trip out of Dún Laoghaire. It was printed in *The
> Irish Times*. As a result, the features editor asked if I would do
> a series of three articles on the fishing industry. I did so, and
> from there on I devoted my time to matters relating to the
> fishing industry, including taking up the development of the
> industry as a political motive. That led on to broadcasting and
> *Fishing News* newspaper articles. Later, I briefed the late, highly
> respected Brendan O'Kelly for the job of chairman and chief
> executive of BIM in the early 1960s. I told him exactly what
> the job was about and what needed to be done. Following his
> appointment in 1962, he proved significantly influential in the
> future development of the industry. One specific criticism I
> had of BIM up to that time was that they sometimes supplied
> boats to skippers that did not have the technical knowledge
> to look after engines or other mechanical items. They had the
> fishing knowledge but didn't have the technical knowledge
> of servicing or maintaining machinery. That aspect of things
> led to lost fishing days and occasionally to flawed criticisms
> of engines and boats. Brendan O'Kelly's appointment trans-
> formed that whole thing.

In 1964, Arthur decided to undertake the far from trivial task of getting an Irish fishing newspaper/magazine off the ground. It would be named *The Irish Skipper*, and its main focus would be the development of the fishing industry. Although he formed a company, being the man he is, Arthur undertook the task virtually single-handed, but settled for the title of 'founding editor'. He recalled the early days of the paper:

To get started, I sent out a few copies and almost immediately subscriptions came in from men of the calibre of Victor Chambers, Annalong, and James McLeod, Killybegs. Those eminent fishermen judged the paper on what they saw and read. I was delighted and knew then the paper was going to be a success. I recall too that Donal O'Driscoll, Castletownbere, contributed greatly. Scarcely an issue went by when he wouldn't phone me and perhaps tell me something of value for the next issue. I was living in Dublin at the time and working in *The Irish Times* at night. Granted, it was a bit of a struggle at first but the only issue that didn't cover its cost was the second one – after that, it just blossomed, each year putting on an increase in paying circulation of about 15 per cent, which was very high! *The Irish Skipper* was printed under contract, with the first run costing £84. It carried about sixty stories per month, written under different names, all of which were pulled out of the phone book of course. I personally edited the entire publication and simply invented all those other names. My experience of working in London tabloid newspapers paid dividends. I applied a lot of the techniques I acquired as a trained newspaper designer there. The main thing was to make the reader read as much and as long as possible. I tended to keep articles short and would never allow two columns to run to the bottom of the page – there always had to be something in between – an advert or whatever. At its peak, the paper was carrying over half on advertising per issue. *The Irish Skipper* was very good to me indeed. Amongst other important necessities, it paid for me to visit numerous different countries where I had opportunities to observe what went on in their fish industries.

As the saying goes, all good things come to an end, and that was so where Arthur's association with *The Irish Skipper* was concerned – he sold it after twenty-seven years.

As part of our varied discussion, we came to talk about one of my hobbyhorses: the BIM 50-footers. Arthur agrees that they played a significant role in the stepping up from half-deckers, but feels that owners in some ports clung on to them for too long. 'Maybe,' he said, 'it was because they suited the drying-out harbours on the east coast.'

Arthur became recognised outside Ireland as a person of standing where the furtherance of fishing and the industry as a whole was concerned, as evidenced by the fact that he acted in a consultative capacity for trawler fleet owners in Skagen, Denmark, and Vigo, Spain. In the 1990s, during the tenure of the last Irish coalition government, he was appointed a direc-tor of BIM. 'I was,' he said, 'motivated by the political side of things, having become disillusioned by politicians.' He went on to explain:

Fianna Fáil controlled BIM for its own motivational pur-poses. This is how they did it. The TDs found out the names of those for whom loans or grants had been sanctioned. While the applicants had not yet been informed of the awards, along went TDs and led recipients to believe that the money had not yet been authorised but that they could fix it for them. I didn't like that sort of thing and fought against it constantly. It was one of the things I didn't like about the Bord or the politi-cians. I can assure you it stopped and that it was not going to happen again.

The Irish Skipper, Issue 1, February 1964. (Courtesy Arthur Reynolds via Inishowen Maritime Museum)

With Brendan O'Kelly's considerable influence on the Irish fishing industry in mind, Arthur went on to say:

Brendan knew the amount of money up-and-coming Killybegs pelagic men were making in the 1970s from fishing 80ft boats, and he pointed out to them that they couldn't stand still; he pushed them in the direction of the big pelagic boats, which of course are now making huge money.

When we moved on to talk about the present state of the fishing industry, this is what Arthur had to say:

> Despite the problems we have, the fact is the demand for fish is increasing. The world sea fish catch is also going up, despite what ignorant critics say about dwindling stocks. There is no question of fishing out stocks. A sheep farmer, if he had the power to run the fish industry, would be able to understand how you crop a stock – do it sensibly and you will constantly have a supply from it.

Reflecting on the discussion years prior to Ireland's entry to the EU, he said:

> I went over for the talks. Spain made the case for maintaining its fishing fleet on the west coast of Ireland. It was Germany that backed Spain and insisted that concessions be given to them. Germany fought Spain's case because it wanted to insure that the Basques, Spain's traditional fishermen, were kept occupied. Why? Because they didn't want the Basques, who were in conflict with the Spanish government, to upset the economy of the country. Why not? Because Germany had turned Spain into an economic colony after the Second World War. German funding was used to build huge hotels by the hundreds, to improve roads, to build bridges and to do all sorts of things to improve their new-found colony. It was German money that did all that, not EU grants. Of course, Ireland had to come into the fold to make the plan work and Germany also saw to that. I know. I spoke to politicians at the time, and I know the people that were negotiating terms.

It would be remiss of me not to refer to some of the 'extra-curricular activities' the octogenarian gentleman has been involved in during his lifetime. He told me he is a practical person who has built two houses with his own hands; sailed widely on yachts around Europe (at times with his great friend Jack Tyrrell); ridden motor bikes for sixty-three years; and has been 'looking carefully' at Irish music for the last twenty-five years.

Married three times, Arthur's current wife, Broghild, is, he said, 'a most interesting Norwegian woman, and a Labour Party politician who sat on the Bergen Harbour Board for sixteen years. The Port of Bergen is the third or fourth richest in Europe.' He also said that his second wife was an archaeologist and that over a thirteen-year period he became involved in many interesting archaeological works. 'It was,' he remarked, 'a lovely change from the sea.'

The obvious question to ask was how he managed to find time to fit so much into one lifetime. He laughed. 'I haven't told you the half of it, but I often wonder myself because I'm not so efficient and my interests are too diverse. I should really be more disciplined in my mind.'

As we were about to call it a day, I enquired about whether there was anything he hadn't done but would like to have done:

Yes, there is. I would like to know more about horses, not horse racing though. I ask people all the time, people who should know, what's the extent of the intelligence of a horse? I always get conflicting answers. I would like to know because horses have had such a massive influence in American and Irish history. There is a big gap in what is known on that topic.

My meeting with Arthur made for a wonderfully interesting afternoon.

6

SPENT A LIFETIME FISHING

Seamus Corr of Skerries, County Dublin

While driving along the shore road in the direction Skerries on a May morning, a line from an old-time melody resurrected itself from depths of my mind – 'One Beautiful Morning in May'. The exquisite vista, enhanced by brilliant sunshine sparkling on the almost perfectly calm water surrounding the offshore low-lying islands, was indeed a joy to behold. But it wasn't to view the scenery that I had made the journey from north Antrim. No, I had come to meet up with Seamus Corr, one of the port's best-known fishermen, now retired. There is little the man, who spent his whole working lifetime at 'the game', doesn't know about it.

His parents on both sides came from the famous Loughshinney fishing families, the Corrs and Wildes. It would have been surprising if Seamus, a teenager in the 1950s, with such strong family fishing traditions, was not to follow in the footsteps of his forebears. He didn't spring any surprises! He started off, as many a young lad with ambitions to one day become a fisherman did, by lobstering during the summer months. When the time came, he took his place in the family queue and waited for a berth to become available on the newly arrived BIM 50-footer *Ros Seán*. That was in the late 1950s. It was a case of waiting for one member of the clan to move on before another could take his place. Yes, fishing on the *Ros Seán* was very much a Corr family affair – Jack was the owner, Georgie was skipper, with Seamus' father, Francis, uncle George, uncle Jack and cousin Paddy as crew. Seamus had to bide his time until Paddy made way. Seamus said, 'That's the way it had been down through the generations.'

Seamus laments the fact that the family-owned boat tradition is virtually a thing of the past. He explained:

> During my lifetime in fishing it has changed from 'a living to a business'. It's all business now. There is little family tradition of

Seamus in the morning sunshine.

boat ownership anymore. Boats are for the most part company-owned; the individual can't finance it nowadays … I enjoyed fishing all my life, it was great, but the fun went out of it for me. I fished for a living; I didn't live to fish. It's the opposite now; they live to fish. Gone are the days when local skippers owned their own trawlers, even though they were only 50- or 56-footers. Now skippers are company employees … Ah, the family tradition of boat ownership was great in the old days. My grandfather on my mother's side, Jim Wilde, had a brand new boat, the *Girl Claire*, built at Killybegs in 1948. My other grandfather on the Corr side at the same time owned the Tyrrell-built *Maid of Loughshinney*, a boat still on the go, having been converted to a pleasure craft.

The early years of Seamus' fishing career were spent on the *Ros Seán*, the beautiful, state-of-the-art, Mevagh-built, varnished-hull 50-footer. She stirred up considerable local interest on her initial arrival at Loughshinney. Seamus recalls that people were up and down all day long to go on board and look the vessel over. So enthralled was his 90-year-old grandfather with the cabin and its comforts that he wanted to stay on board for ever. He refused to go home for his dinner! Nowadays million-pound boats arrive at port virtually unnoticed.

Seamus recalls his years on the *Ros Seán*, when it was skippered by Georgie Corr, with great fondness. 'We did very well, though we had the occasional disappointment.' He recalled one particular trip to Morecombe Bay, which had amusing aspects to it, but ended frustratingly. He described the 'adventure' as follows:

> I was still young and the older men were in charge. Other local boats had been fishing in the bay so we set off to join them, not really knowing where we were going. The crew had not fished there previously. The sum total of navigational aids aboard was

a compass. I'm not sure how long we were at sea but myself and another young chap, Stephen Attley [later owner of the 56-footer *Morning Star*] were down in the cabin when a call came from the skipper [Georgie] to come up as it was time to shoot. I asked Georgie how he knew we were at the fishing grounds, to which he replied, I don't know but I can see John Henry [Doyle] in the *Conquest* over there, so we must be in the right place. Another member of the Corr clan, Eddie, had made special tail ends of about 100mm mesh for the trawl. Having shot the net, Stephen and I returned to the cabin. Ten to fifteen minutes later, Georgie again called for us to come on deck. The trawl had to be foul of rocks or something, I thought to myself, it's nowhere near long enough shot! When we asked what was wrong, the skipper said he wasn't sure but something was amiss. Being on unknown ground, he felt that we should attempt to board the net. That we did. To our amazement, the tail end was full of massive plaice! With our hands ripped to pieces from handling the fish from the first and subsequent hauls, we headed for home with 250 boxes of the finest plaice you ever saw.

Alas, there ended the happy part of the story because a glut of plaice in the Dublin market meant that the fish failed to find a buyer – they were dumped. Instead of a lucrative return for the boatload of prime fish, the owner, my uncle Jack, received a bill for expense incurred. He personally delivered the bad news to us and in way of lessening the blow gave us each £20 out of his own pocket.

Following his years on the *Ros Seán*, Seamus was in a position to invest in his own boat. He looked around for a suitable vessel. On the market was the *Ard Finnian*, a BIM 56-footer, built at the Killybegs yard in 1962. Having been re-engined and in good condition, 'a lovely little boat', Seamus purchased her in 1972. Now, all these years later, the memory of his purchase prompted him to tell me of the very first time he saw the *Ard Finnian*:

We were fishing outside the Rockabill [in the *Ros Seán*, I pre-
sume] and there fishing beside us was this 'beauty' with mizzen
set belonging to Paddy Sugrue, a Kerryman, then based at
Howth. We were all looking at this beautiful boat when the
older men on the crew came to the conclusion that no matter
how fine, she was too big for fishing that ground. If they could
see the size of boats trawling there now, some up to 120ft, I
wonder what they would think.

Immediately following the acquisition of the *Ard Finnian*
(D402), Seamus engaged in seine netting for six months or so.
Then he changed over to prawn trawling and that particular
type of fishing was to be his mainstay for the remainder of
his career. He recalled that in those days cod were also very
plentiful in the spring. Where the cod later disappeared to is
another story, which he returned to later in our chat.

So successful was Seamus with the *Ard Finnian* that a few
years later he sold her to Michael Collins of Kilkeel and in
1976 had a new boat, the 65ft cruiser-stern, very eye-catching
Francis Maria (D441), built at Maritime, Cobh, County Cork.
The building cost of around £250,000 was whittled down
to around £130,000 for the purchaser, after grants came into
play. That was very good for a new boat. The arrival of the
Francis Maria on the fishing scene coincided with the closure
of the Celtic Sea herring fishery and very poor prices being
paid for prawns. She paired for a time, herring-fishing off the
Isle of Man, with Frank Rogan's Skerries-based *Mary Lorraine*
(D544), another Cobh-built 65-footer, but with a transom
stern. Like many other owners, paying off the outstanding
debt on the boat became financially non-viable for Seamus.
With repossessions rife, he looked around for a buyer and
believes he was fortunate to meet well-established fishermen
Frank and Joe Doherty, of Kincasslagh, County Donegal – 'I
was one of the lucky ones; I got a good family with plenty of
money to buy the *Francis Maria*.'

With the *Francis Maria* gone, Seamus joined the crew of Georgie Rogan's Skerries boat, the 63ft *Carnown Bay* (D590). He did six months or so on her, but was always on the lookout for a suitable boat to buy. His quest took him to Howth, where, on the advice of one John Dixon, an elderly shipwright, he became interested in a particular BIM 56-footer, the *Ard Rathain* (D262). Fitted with a brand-new Gardner engine, the 1956 Mevagh-built boat was in great condition – 'a grand little boat'. Was she up for sale or not? At first, her owner, Baltimore man Pat Harrington, seemed uncertain. However, Seamus, along with his brother Frank, decided to pursue the matter. Frank rang Pat, who, after some hesitation, decided to sell the boat. All of that took place in 1979, the year Seamus and Frank became owners of the *Ard Rathain*.

The *Loughshinney*.

During the years Seamus fished the *Ard Rathain*, he had some memorable catches of cod. He reflected on one such landing in 1980:

I love horse racing, so Olivia and I went to Fairyhouse for the Irish Grand National one Easter Monday. I believe that during the course of the day, and night, I over-indulged in the hard stuff, so much so that I wasn't feeling at all well the following morning! Going to sea had very little appeal on that particular Tuesday. However, old habits die hard, so where else would one go to see what was happening but to the pier and perhaps a visit to Joe May's? It was then around 10 a.m. Some boats were beginning to head off for the fishing grounds. I must have been coming around a bit at that stage, or maybe I was feeling a little guilty, but for whatever reason I decided to go too. While the other boats headed out east, I went north towards where a boat was fishing. It turned out to be the beautiful, Tyrrell-built, 70ft *Shelmalier* (WD63). Floating alongside her was a big bag of cod. I immediately got on the blower and informed the skippers of other Skerries boats that it looked as if cod were on the go. Some believed I was having them on, but Peter Campbell in the *Ard Gillen* (D453) decided that there was something in what I was saying and headed over our way.

At the same time, we came across the *Ton Ton Louis* (D488), skippered by Paddy McGrath, heading for Howth and down to the numbers. He had been fishing over the weekend. We went on down and picked up the spot where the cod were. The sounder went black! We shot a prawn net and towed through the marking. When it came up it was balloon-like – 180 boxes of cod and 20 boxes of whiting! Peter, likewise, who had also shot at that stage, boarded around 200 boxes. A second shot yielded us a further 140 boxes. Peter had something similar. The two boats, *Ard Rathain* and *Ard Gillen*, were filled from stem to stern with cod. Fortunately the sea was as smooth as glass as we made our way back to Skerries. Otherwise the fish would have fallen out over the rails. Between the two 56-footers we landed over 700 boxes, mostly of cod, and all caught in prawn nets. It was almost unbelievable. The following day there wasn't a cod to be caught in the same spot. A huge shoal must have come in to spawn on the soft bottom. Most of the cod caught were females. Unfortunately once again poor prices at the Dublin market took much of the gloss off the landings. We got little or nothing for them; lack of worthwhile markets at the time led to disastrous situations. Occasionally fish completely failed to sell. It happened at a time when up to eight lorry loads of fish, mostly whiting, left Skerries pier four or five nights a week for the Dublin market.

In time, the *Ard Rathain* was sold to Dick Deasy, Union Hall. There was then a short interlude in the Corr fishing activities before they once again began to look around for another boat. This time they settled for the 1960, Scotch-built, 55-footer, *Boy Stephen* (D656). She was bought from a Kilkeel owner. The Corrs replaced the 114hp Gardner with a 280hp/209kW Volvo Penta. She was a fine boat that served the Corr family well before they sold her on to Union Hall man, Dick Deasy.

During the course of our chat, Seamus described prawn fishing as the mainstay of much of his fishing career. As such, I asked how he remembered the prawn scene over the years. This is what he had to say:

It was of course tails only up to around the mid-1970s. There was no market for whole prawns until Derek Younger, the man who built the Red Sail processing factory at Clogherhead, started buying them. We supplied prawns to him over many years when he worked at Seabourne and Cullens. That was previous to his opening the plant at Clogherhead. Currently there is huge money to be made out of landing whole prawns.

I'm afraid that was not the case in our days; we got loads of prawns but prices were poor.

While cod, whiting and haddock are now as rare as hen's teeth off the east coast, prawns have endured. In spite of fairly constant and intensive fishing, they have not disappeared. I wondered if Seamus had an explanation:

> Well, scientists have certainly not come up with conclusive answers. Theories, yes, but nothing concrete. It has been suggested that equal proportions of male and female of the species off the east coast is a factor, i.e. they breed in abundance. This is not always the case as ratios of male to female have elsewhere been recorded as low as one to nine. While that explanation may have substance, it is unlikely to be the whole answer ... Years ago I met a prawn researcher who openly admitted that in spite of extensive tests little is known of prawn behavioural patterns.

Seamus recalled an occasion, years ago, around the months of May or June, when prawns temporarily disappeared from the coast:

> We had been fishing them fairly heavily for a good number of years. The old men of the day said we had overfished and that the prawns were gone forever. Right enough there was some concern when none were caught over a few months. However, a little later a southerly gale blew up; I'll always remember it was around the time a world regatta was to take place in Skerries. When the gale abated we headed off down the bay [towards Clogherhead] to give the prawns a go. *Loughshinney* skipper, Christy Plunkett, was first to haul. Attempts to lift the gear aboard were proving unusually problematic. Indeed, it was often a difficult job in those days as we had no proper lifting gear. However, on this occasion it was exceptionally so. Eventually, with help, he managed to

land a huge bagful of prawns on the deck. That signalled their return! We had forty boxes of tails for that one day's fishing. The old men were wrong on that occasion. As for overfishing, if they were around now to witness multimillion-pound boats fishing prawns day in, day out, I don't know what they would think.

Having discussed prawn endurance, my next question was why have cod, whiting and haddock, each so plentiful locally at one time, virtually reached extinction? Seamus' first words were, 'It's amazing where the cod went from here.' He continued:

We did overfish them in later years. I got some fine shots of cod. It was different in the 1950s and early '60s when I fished on the *Ros Seán*. Then we only fished from Monday to Friday, and usually a short day on Friday, maybe just one tow. There was no way that the old men would fish on a Sunday – it was definitely a day of rest. You washed the boat down, tidied up and checked gear on Friday evening and Saturday. On Saturday evening the boat was put on the moorings and that's where she stayed until Monday morning. Over the years, that scenario changed. The arrival of the three-bridled net and boats from the south that fished the cod twenty-four hours a day, seven days a week, took its toll. For a while we continued to work the five-day week but it came to a stage where we had no option but to join the others. Then you had French trawlers and English 'Sputnik trawlers' [steel-built, 75ft, 200hp mini-trawlers] all catching loads of cod. I suppose the concentrated, nonstop fishing must have cleaned them out. Now with the restrictions a few are returning.

As in the case of cod, Seamus said:

It used to be that you could almost catch whiting with a bucket. Now you wouldn't get enough for your dinner if you

were out there all day. We landed loads and loads of whiting
and haddock here. Now there's none. Pelagic fishing hasn't
helped either. While we worked bottom nets, the pelagic boats
use huge nets that can be raised and lowered in the water.
There is no hiding place for the fish.

The setting up of a fishmeal factory at Mornington, County
Louth, in years gone by was something that should never have
happened, according to Seamus. It provided a ready market on
the doorstep for all sizes and varieties of fish, the long-term
consequences of which had to be detrimental to sustainability.
He said, 'I landed fish there myself but the whole thing was
wrong. We were catching everything, no matter how small. It
ruined fishing in the whole "bay". It was in the 1970s and
there was no control on mesh size at that time.'

Seamus made reference to the many boats that he, sometimes along with his brother Frank, had ownership of. Included
were the *Ard Finnian* (D402), *Francis Maria* (D441), *Ard Rathain*
(D262) and *Boy Stephen* (D656). Well, there were still more to
come! Around 1988, the Corrs decided on yet another BIM
56-footer. The 1958, Mevagh-built *Ard Mhuire* (D5) was to be
the third of that particular breed skippered by Seamus. She
was purchased from Michael Doherty, Greencastle, and was
to prove a very successful boat. Seamus said, 'We did well with
her, very well. We fished her for fifteen years. By then she was
getting long in the tooth.'

While the *Ard Mhuire* is now long gone, Seamus still has a
few lasting memories of her, but here is one that surpasses all
others; one he will never forget. He described the incident in
question as follows:

We were hauling the trawl one nasty, dirty day. My young-
est son James was standing near the rail. The boat was rolling
and tossing and as the net came up the chain snapped, hitting
James and causing him to overbalance. He fell overboard. It

took an instant for me to realise what had actually happened;
then I saw James in the water. I could see he was trying to
swim towards us. We closed in on him fairly quickly, but, try
as we might, with a big swell causing the boat to lift and fall
erratically, we just couldn't get hold of him. We were greatly
hindered by splashing water coming up over the side of the
boat and parts of our fishing gear getting in the way. As luck
would have it, personnel on a nearby Irish Navy vessel became
aware of our desperate situation and quickly had a boarding
dingy speeding in our direction. In little or no time, the navy
crew members lifted James from the water and took him back
to their vessel. None the worse for his experience, he was later
landed in Skerries. I will never forget the agony of those minutes James was in the water and of our helplessness at not being
able to get him back on board. It makes me tremble to think
about it to this day. Had I lost the boy, I would never again have
put my foot on a boat.

With the *Ard Mhuire* in retirement, the Corrs turned their
attention to a bigger boat, the *Adastra* (G485). They purchased
her from Bertie Ahern, not the ex-Taoiseach, as I momentar-
ily concluded, but a man of the same name from the Aran
Islands. By then, the new century was well and truly established. With it came a term, 'Code of Practice', which was to
have far-reaching implications for many fishermen. The Corrs
experienced its implications in the early days of *Adastra* ownership by 'putting her through at the time'. Having fished
her for three and a half years, what Seamus describes as 'the
more serious Code of Practice' came into being. It was decision time – should they or shouldn't they go ahead with the
survey? Eventually they went ahead, even though it was costing a lot of money. The outcome was that a major keel job was
required and the 230 Gardner engine also needed an overhaul.
There was too much expense involved. Seamus and Frank
were no longer young men. The way fishing was going, it was

unlikely that they would want to delve again into a world largely unknown to fishermen of yesteryear.

Now, could it be that the very long fishing tradition established by generation after generation of the Corr family was about to come to an end? The answer to that question is no. With the *Adastra* tied up, Seamus and his son, James, kept an eye out for another boat. Word filtered through that a suitable boat might be coming up for sale. The O'Flahertys (Kilmore Quay) were about put a steel-hulled 48ft trawler named *Our Tracey* on the market. With the boat lying in Howth, Seamus suggested to James that he should go and look her over. Satisfied with what he saw, James spoke to Denis O'Flaherty and a deal was made. She arrived at Skerries in February 2012. With her name changed to the *Sheriff* (Seamus' nickname of many years), skippered by James, and with his brother Frank (Francis) on the crew, she was fully engaged in prawn fishing when I called at the Corr home. Seamus is obviously overjoyed that James has carried on the family fishing tradition. He is equally pleased that James' older brother Frank, having done his skipper's ticket, and spent some years working as a chef, has returned home to make his living as a fisherman. Satisfaction, too, is derived from the fact that a cousin, Georgie Corr, fishes the Price-owned *Primrose* (DA93). Long may the Corr family fishing tradition continue!

Seamus reflected briefly on the number of trawlers now fishing out of Skerries in comparison to when he had the *Francis Maria* back in 1976. 'At that time,' he said, 'there were thirty-five boats here. I remember there were eleven boats abreast of each other at the pier and all standing at low water because of the tidal nature of the harbour. Now I think there are only three Wilde-owned twin riggers and our James' little boat.'

Because of my interest in the BIM 56-footers, I thought there could be no one better to ask about them than the man who had, over the years, owned three of them – *Ard Finnian*, *Ard Rathain* and *Ard Mhuire*. His immediate reply was:

> I thought they were the best sea boats ever. However, they were not all the same. The *Ard Finnian*, for example, with a gross tonnage of thirty-eight, exceeded that of the Mevagh-built *Ard Mhuire* by the considerable amount of three. This begs the question, if all BIM 56-footers were built from the same plans, why was the gross tonnage not a constant? Well, I decided to educate myself a little on the topic of gross tonnage. By definition, gross tonnage is a measure of volume inside a vessel and is calculated by means of a complex mathematical formula. It is a unitless index and the standard most often used to define a vessel. It should not, however, be confused with terms such as displacement [mass] or deadweight. Much of the information used in the calculating formula is dependent on measurements of areas taken humanly inside the vessel. I was reliably informed that those measurements may not always be taken from exactly from the same reference points, or indeed with the same level of accuracy. Those factors could have a considerable bearing on the final tonnage figure. It is also the possible that the positioning of bulkheads and pieces of machinery within the vessel may cause discrepancies.

Seamus believes that Paddy Sugrue, original owner of the *Ard Finnian*, had herring fishing very much on his mind when she was being built and probably had his eye on maximum hold capacity.

Seamus went on to say, 'The men who built those boats were proud men: the finished article had to be right; there was pride in every timber that went into them.' With reference to Tyrrell-built boats, he said, 'They were fantastic, boats such as the *Brian Og* (D531), and the *Thomas McDonagh* (D509); they were the pride of the fleet.'

As I was about to bid the genial 66-year-old Skerries man adieu, he hung his head for a moment and said, 'Over the years at sea we had a few sad days too. None more so than when my cousins, Joe and Paul Wilde, separately drowned when out fishing. Joe was on the *Savanna* and Paul was on the *Sabrina*. Those were terrible times. May God rest their souls.'

7

A MAN FOR ALL SEASONS

George Gallagher of Inver, County Donegal

When it was first suggested that, Inver man, George Gallagher, had a great maritime story to tell, he was unknown to me. However, a few enquires about his identity quickly revealed that I was in the minority in this regard. Yes, it seemed that George, widely described as one of life's gentlemen, was known not only in his native Donegal but also in fishing ports right around the Irish coast. When I contacted him to arrange a meeting, the only stipulation he made was, 'Make sure to allow plenty of time when you come because I have lots to tell you.' This did indeed prove to be the case!

On a fine mid-April morning, kindly escorted by my good friend Michael O'Boyle, of Mountcharles, I arrived at the home of George and his wife Bridget. The attractively restored family farmhouse is serenely situated at Fanaghans on the western shore of Inver Bay. Across the way, protruding into the greater expanse of Donegal Bay, is Doorin Point.

Michael and I stood for a moment to take in the magnificence of the scenic surroundings. Soon we were joined by George, who extended a warm welcome to us.

Michael headed off, as George and I went inside. It quickly became clear that the man sitting opposite me was indeed 'a man for all seasons'. Initially, the purpose of my visit was to learn about a particular inshore fishing technique that has been utilised in and around Inver Bay for as long as anyone can remember. But there was more, much more! Initiatives, representations and local projects in general had featured hugely in the life and times of this genial and outgoing man.

George, then approaching his mid-seventies, was born and reared in the village of Inver. Following in the footsteps of his forbearers he became a man of the sea at an early age. His childhood memory of fishing activities in Inver was of seeing men who went to sea at daybreak returning on dark winter evenings with baskets of lines under their arms. Leading the

George Gallagher rigging his boat.

way, as they passed the door of the Gallagher family home, would be a crew member carrying a hurricane lamp. George says, 'While growing up I was always around boats.' As a 15-year-old, he replaced his ailing uncle in a herring driftnet yawl. 'It was,' he recalls, 'a tough business rowing to the fishing grounds in an open yawl on winter nights, shooting nets, waiting, hauling, clearing, rowing back home and landing the catch. Still I enjoyed it. Fish were plentiful and that in turn generated a great deal of activity in and around the village.'

Reflecting on life of the 1940s and '50s in the Inver neighbourhood, he says, 'It was a good community in every way.' He believes the trauma suffered by the people of south Donegal during the years of the great famine left an indelible mark, so much so, that it filtered down and had an effect on people's way of life in his young days. People believed in self-sufficiency; they cut their own peat, grew corn and potatoes, reared their own hens and chickens, stored up salt fish. Most had a cow or two and a couple of calves, corn was milled nearby and they had plenty of straw for thatching and flour for baking. George says:

> They had hay for the cows, a stack of turf for the fire and no mortgage. A bad winter didn't worry anyone too much. Importantly, everyone had time for everyone else. The occasional jealousy or disagreement that arose for one reason and another only lasted until illness or death befell a family, then all was forgotten. It was a good way of life! We cycled to dances and without the luxuries and conveniences of today we enjoyed ourselves as teenagers and young men. People were happy, happier than they are today, I believe.

Common surnames in the close-knit Inver and Port communities were that of: Rose, McHugh, Gallagher, Furey, Toland, Meehan, Keeney, Ward, Haughey, Kennedy, McAndrew, Friel, Murphy, McDyre, Tierney, Cunningham, Montgomery, Fisher and Battle.

Now that I had established George's background and
his way of thinking, it was time to learn something of the
inshore fishing technique that was extensively carried out in
the Inver/south Donegal area up to the 1990s, and, which
he believes is unique. Nowhere in his travels around the
Irish coast or elsewhere has he seen or heard of this particular modus operandi being employed. With slight variations
in mesh and net size, the method has long been used in the
catching of salmon, mackerel and sprat. The prerequisites
were a yawl, oars or an outboard engine, and a net. George
stated that, 'This type of fishing is not to be found anywhere
else in the world. It's completely unique to south Donegal
and particularly to the Inver area.' George, as I understand it, was referring to a variation on the draft netting of
salmon, mackerel and sprat, which involved an element of
purse seining. The yawls originally used were the traditional
wooden type of the area, but by the 1990s, fibreglass boats,
modelled on traditional boats, were in use and proved to be
very successful.

Tightening the ring.

Let's first consider salmon fishing. The procedure began with a crew of five or six aboard a 24ft yawl, moored fairly close to the local strand. A sharp lookout was kept for salmon jumping in the water. A sighting was the cue to get under-way. The skipper manoeuvred the boat into a position for the net 'shooting' to commence. The net used was about 200 yards long and about 20 yards deep at the centre. It was made in such a way that it formed a bag or purse as it was being hauled. During 'shooting', the boat moved in a circular fashion so that the net formed 'a ring', thereby surrounding the fish. Once 'the ring' was completed, the crew began to hand-haul the net into the boat, with two men on the top rope (cork rope) and two men on the soles (foot rope). As a result, the ring formed decreased in circumference and the bag or purse began to form as the soles were hauled aboard. However, an opening between the sole ropes remained for some time and the chances of fish escaping from the net had to be curtailed. In order to minimise the escape, a crew member used an oar to fill the gap – that is, an oar was swept from side to side through the water in front of the opening in an effort to divert the fish towards the centre. With the soles and net centre aboard, the fish were safely trapped in the 'bag'. Any remaining yarn in the water was hauled in and the salmon manually lifted from the 'bag'. An anchor slipped over the stern quarter of the boat opposite the net-hauling side prevented the boat from 'falling down'.

George went on to point out that:

Salmon ringing is an extremely skilled operation. From start to finish, each individual on the boat has to know his job to a tee. It has to be borne in mind that five or six men were all working at the same time in a confined area while the net was being hauled. Meanwhile the sea was lapping the gunwale of the 24ft yawl and net hauling adjustments were necessary to ensure the gunwale stayed above water. From the time salmon

were first spotted jumping, the man responsible for selecting
the most advantageous position to set about making the ring
had to take into account of the direction in which the fish
were swimming and the speed at which they are travelling. Just
as important was that the hauling of the net was carried out
in a well-rehearsed fashion to ensure that it came in evenly
throughout the operation.

Once landed, salmon were boxed, iced and made ready for
transporting by rail to Dublin. The first stage of the journey
involved the narrow-gauge line that began at Killybegs and
ran via Inver to Strabane, County Tyrone.

Mackerel- and sprat-fishing procedures were, with some variations, largely similar to the procedure employed for the fishing
of salmon. It had to be taken into account that mackerel are very
fast movers and, as a result, were caught only close to the shore
in reasonably shallow water. George also emphasised that meshing had to be kept to a minimum in order to avoid tangling,
which made handling the net difficult. To that end, fish were
forced in as far as possible towards small meshes at the centre
and kept away from the outside, where mesh size was larger.

In the sprat-fishing operation, when the 'ring' was formed, a
man sitting at the front of the boat plunged a tapered wooden
pole of around 15ft in length down through the water. If fish
were 3 to 4 yards from the surface, contact with them resulted
in a pressure being exerted on the pole. From the degree of
pressure exerted, an experienced 'pole man' was able to ascer-
tain the position of the fish and how plentiful they were. The
latter was of considerable importance because hauling a sprat
net, which was much heavier than its salmon or mackerel nets,
was very hard work. Fish therefore had to be present in sufficient quantity to justify the effort. A pole in the hands of an
experienced man was invaluable.

The sprat net-hauling operation is a delicate procedure,
requiring skill and dexterity:

As the bag floated on the surface and the sprat become visible, great care had to be taken that each man hauled his portion level with the other, in order to keep the bag in the proper shape as it came in beside the boat. In the case of large catches, with up to seven tons to deal with, if not handled properly, a disaster could easily occur. With the bag secured beside the boat, the fish could either be transferred to small individual bags, or floated ashore if the tide conditions were favourable. Floating a large bagful of sprat ashore was a tricky operation. The boat would be listing acutely throughout. Without the luxury of a pier, fish had to be landed at the water's edge on a nearby strand. The level of skill involved in the whole sprat-fishing operation was incredible. It was often a difficult and laborious task but one which was carried out with a sense of satisfaction and enthusiasm. It's a skill that has been handed down from generation to generation. As records show, it goes back to the seventeenth century.

He further recalled that the actual landing of a sprat catch was a whole community effort. Apparently everyone that was free, and even some who were not so free, came to help. Even the local publican was known to lend a hand. With the catch having been successfully 'grounded' on the strand, the job of moving it to an area where it could be boxed and iced commenced. That having been done, a load was ready for transportation by lorry to Dublin, from whence it was shipped to England. There, the British Fish Canning Co., based at Leeds, was a big-time buyer.

Sadly, while some sprats have been landed in recent years the quantities are minimal in comparison to that of years gone by. The magnitude of the quantities of sprat landed at Inver in former times can be gleaned from the fact that George recalls counting 2,100 4-stone boxes ready for transporting at the end of one particular day's fishing. He also personally remembers upwards of forty boats, some hailing from the local area, others from St John's Point, fishing in the bay. For the most part, the boats used were pre-1990s McDonald-built

Landing the catch at Inver Strand.

(Moville/Greencastle) yawls. Only a single yawl now remains, which George describes as, 'the last working yawl in Ireland'.

Mention of those boats prompted him to relate a story involving a yawl named *St Christopher*.

> She was once used as a lifeboat. In the mid-1960s, on a very stormy day, two men set out to sail across Donegal Bay towards Mullaghmore on the Sligo coast. Out in the middle of the bay the boat capsized, throwing the occupants into the water. Local men ashore observed the incident and, realising the seriousness of the situation, immediately set about launching the *St Christopher*. Powered by an outboard engine, with oars as backup, they made their way in difficult sea conditions towards the capsized boat. On arrival at the scene, it was immediately obvious that the men in the water were about to give up the ghost; they were suffering from exposure and exhaustion. With symptoms of hypothermia in evidence, speed was of the essence. Working quickly in rough seas, the *St Christopher* was manoeuvred into a position from which the men were

plucked from the water just in the nick of time. Two lives were saved. I have very special memories of the *St Christopher*.

While George remembers more than forty boats fishing in Inver Bay during the 1960s, an extract from the Registry of Fishing Vessels on the Coast of Ireland, dated 5 January 1844, puts the significance of Inver as a fishing centre at that time into context. It reads, 'There are about 550 boats connected with Inver Bay port, averaging from 1½ to 8 tons each. There are generally about 3,000 fishermen employed in the fishing season.' A further extract from the same document refers to a fishery pier at Inver Bay:

> The winter fishing (which I am informed was very good) is entirely lost, as, in case of a storm, there is no safe harbour nearer than 6 miles from the fishing grounds. There is at present the remains of an old quay adjoining a small valley called the Port, opposite to which the fishing is principally carried on, and which, if rebuilt, and extended but a little, would be of the greatest benefit, as well to those engaged in fishing as to any vessels which might put in from stress of weather, there being 12 feet at high water at the point of the present old quay.

Further mention of the proposed structure in another part of the text states that, 'It would answer all the purposes of the fishermen, and even for coasters of 120 tons burthen.'

Alas, the above recommendation, penned by one R. St George Johnston to the Tidal Harbours Commission, fell on deaf ears. While it was made known that some private funds could be raised, and that a great deal of expense would be saved by the labour of fishermen, who, it was said, 'would assist at the work for a certain time most cheerfully', no such quay was ever built. Fishermen had to resign themselves to using boats that could be hauled in and out of the sea with comparative ease. Yawls were the obvious choice. Had the proposed project materialised, George's belief is that Inver would have become the Killybegs of today. Alas, on the contrary, apart from the occasional pleasure craft, the only boats now seen on the bay are the few that engage in fishing meagre sprat shoals, and those of the creel men working along the shore.

When I asked if fishing had been his main means if livelihood, he replied:

> Ah no, it was for many years but it wasn't constant enough. Remember, I had a wife and six children to support. I did various bits and pieces of work with the County Council and anything else suitable that turned up. That was the case until 1967 when Bridport-Gundry (Ireland), Ltd., Killybegs, first opened its doors. It was a business that presented a permanent employment opportunity to me. It was vital that I made the most of it. Initially I was one of a three-man operation: the late James McLeod, a manager, and myself. James was an exceptional director. I was to function mainly as an out-and-about salesman, supplying gear to inshore fishermen and retail outlets around the coastline. Not having travelled a great deal up until then, it could be said I was a bit of a 'country boy'. I did, however, have a good background in traditional netting, which was backed up by two and a half years' experience at the Killybegs branch of a prestigious Danish net-making company. I knew the job would be a big challenge but I was determined to make a success of it.

George smiled as he went on to relate what he referred to as going 'down memory lane on the Gundry trips'. He said:

> Initially cold-calling wasn't always pleasant, but I soon got to know a number of top-class people involved in the fishing scene. Once established, I never looked back. I remember Burtonport to be the first place I got a foothold in. At the

time the harbour was so filled with boats that, at first glance, so plentiful were masts it could be mistaken for a forest. Alas, today Burtonport harbour is largely deserted and business at the once-busy nearby shops and hostelries that have managed to survive is but a pale shadow of yesteryear. However, that's another story, one that scarcely bears thinking about.

In his early days on the road, George recalls that he set up a sale-or-return fishing gear store within the Burtonport Fisherman's Co-operative framework. Joe Boyle, better known as Joe Joe Phil, had retired from fishing the 56ft *Ard Chroine* to run the Co-op. George recalls that Joe Joe was an extremely busy man. So busy was he at times that it was normal to see him trying to serve three customers all at once. Yet, he says, 'regardless of how hard pressed he was, Joe Joe always managed to make a joke or raise a laugh about something or other – a grand man of whom I have great memories.'

Once George found his feet as a travelling salesman, the he could be found dealing with clients anywhere around the coast. In County Donegal, he could be at Bunbeg, where the Sweeneys, O'Donnels and Gillespies were great customers, or maybe further north with the O'Briens and Colls at Horn Head. Meeting up with gentlemen such as John Parry and the late Bertie Robinson was indeed a great pleasure. At Downings he was always sure of a cuppa and a few yarns with the late Hugh McBride and his wife Jenny. George, shaking his head, said, 'Ah, but the years have taken their toll on many of the great fishermen on the Fanad Peninsula that were so special to me'. With obvious sadness, he went on to say, 'There was Stephen Coll, the man with his cap a little bit to "the south-west", Din Friel, who knew all there was to know about inshore fishing and could build you a fine currach, and then there was the "holy man" and great fisherman, Jim McGroarty.'

At Greencastle he had lots of customers, too many to mention, all of whom he regarded as friends. Some he worked very closely with, including were the Kelly brothers, good fishermen and great net workers who did work for Gundry's at that time. At Greencastle also he worked closely with Pat McLaughlin, a man who spent over twenty years fishing before retiring to start up what has become the extremely successful Carrymacarry Networks Ltd. He went on to say, 'No trip to the Lough Foyle side village would be complete without calling on Cavanagh Nets Ltd.'

With so many customers in County Donegal, I was beginning to think that George wouldn't have time to cover the remainder of the coastline. How wrong I was! Two calls further afield were the north-coast ports of Ballycastle and Cushendun, both in County Antrim. At Ballycastle he referred to his friend, the late, big Sean Morton – a great salmon man – while at Cushendun it was Paddy McNeill that he called on. Across the country, on the Sligo coast, the O'Neills of Enniscrone availed of his services. In County Mayo, travelling west from Killala, he met up with hard workers and good fishermen such as the late Pat (Rua) O'Reilly, Chris Flannery and the O'Donnels at Porturlin. A visit to Belmullet was, George says, 'always a treat. You could smell Mary Geraghty's homemade buns a mile out of town.' Mary apparently made lobster pots, which she covered on the surface of a billiard table. At Achill Island, amongst those he met up with were the Sweeneys, the Corrigans, the Levelles, and Brendan Murray, the manager who worked so hard for West Mayo Fishermen's Co-op. Cleggan, on the Galway coast, was one of his favourite calls and there, among others, he met up with the now deceased Wallace brothers, Patrick, Martin and Willie – highly respected fishermen. Then there were the men he called on at Letterfrack, Clifden, Ballyconneely, Roundstone, Carna, Rossaveal and Galway – many characters and real gentleman all along the way. While some of them might have been described as small-time fishermen, they were highly successful in their own right. 'The Galway area was like a second home to me. It would be remiss of me not to mention the late Pat Jennings. He was one of the great fishing and sailing experts on the west coast. It was such a pleasure to meet up with him.'

As George continued his southwards trail, he called on customers on the County Clare coast, notably at Carrigaholt, before continuing on to County Kerry. At Dingle, he says, 'You might meet the very well-known Benny Moore, who was sure to have many questions to ask and complaints to make. At Ballydavid I looked forward to meeting the equally well-known T.P. O'Counihan.'

The next port of call was Castletownbere, mention of which brought a hint of sadness to George's voice. He went on to explain that on his many trips there, a workmate, Jimmy Cunningham of Killybegs, accompanied him. Apparently the two men began their employment at Gundry's within a year of each other and became very close friends. Alas, Jimmy's untimely death at the age of 56 was like the loss of a family

The memorial stone at Ardaghey Graveyard, County Donegal.

member. Mention of the early death of Castletownbere man, Frank Downey, whom George described as a 'real gentleman', also evoked sadness.

Moving east along the south coast, the intrepid Gundry's man called on Kieran Cotter at Baltimore. 'Kieran,' he says, 'was a great friend of mine. Initially I met him at an exhibition in Galway and subsequently sold him the first fishing gear he retailed. His telephone number was Baltimore 106. We once travelled together to an exhibition in Copenhagen.' Mention of that particular trip caused George to laugh heartily as he recalled a remark made by Kieran whilst the two of them were out for a late evening stroll in the Danish capital. They observed 'a lady of the night' on a street corner. She was approached by a succession of prospective clients, each of whom, after a short conversation, walked on. Then along came a chap who likewise spoke briefly to her and off the pair went. Mimicking the West Cork accent, George related Kieran's remark on what they had seen, 'That's the way, boy! It just shows if you hold out long enough for a good price you'll eventually get it.'

That George quickly established himself as an adept and valued salesman with Bridport–Gundry goes without saying. Having served thirty-three years as technical sales manager for Inshore Fisheries, he retired from the company in 2000. Extracts from text penned in 2006 by Mr Richard McCormick, manager of Bridport–Gundry (Killybegs) in 1979, gives a telling insight into the character that George was – and indeed is:

> George was sales manager for the small boat inshore sector at Gundry's, a position which took him all round the coast into numerous small ports and landing places that few people knew about, with the result that he became an invaluable asset to the company to which he was totally loyal and committed until his retirement. His ability to sell was legendary. He had an

uncanny knack of spotting a full wallet even if secreted under many layers of clothing. When things around the factory were quiet, he would load up the van with goods and disappear over the horizon and return a few days later laden with cash, more orders and a beaming smile of contentment. Much of his selling prowess was due to the extremely high opinion in which his customers held him. He knows just about everything there is to know about inshore fishing gear and techniques, and he also knows everyone on the Irish coast, north and south. He was welcomed wherever he went with a cup and a good chat, out of which inevitably a sale would arise.

George's sense of good humour and wit was legendary.

As a young man in my first senior managerial position, George was a godsend and I began more and more to appreciate the importance of his personal touch in sales and to rely on his judgement as to what would and would not sell. He was my 'spiritual advisor' on matters inshore and largely because of his efforts the specialist inshore market was an extremely profitable part of Gundry's operations in the early 1980s. He taught me the importance of haggling and timing, when and how to cut a deal, when to extend credit and when to insist on cash or call in the debt when fishing was good, all of which was instinctive to him.

He is still well remembered on the coast as I find whenever I meet fishermen, reflecting the high esteem in which those who came in contact with him still hold him. One can take George's sense of honesty, decency, kindness and sincerity for granted and there are few I could say that measure up so highly to those exceptionally valuable personal traits.

Glowing remarks indeed from a man who knows George well. George recalls his years at Gundry's with a great sense of satisfaction:

When I first went on the road, there was definitely a demand for inshore fishing gear. Initially some customers were unsure as to which type of gear best suited their particular kind of fishing. To help out, I would go down the west coast or wherever, stay for a few days, and set-up what could be called informal workshops. Interested fishermen came along. As best I could, I set up gear and showed how them how to rig their own. I had a fair idea of what they needed, but I didn't push it too much. As time went by, fishermen realised that I was there to help, knew what I was talking about, and gradually saw me as one of their own. Local outlets selling gear were very thin on the ground when I started. I saw the need to do something about that. Gradually I got people interested: shop owners and others who were prepared to rent a small store or shed from which to work. Such outlets proved a great success. Ah, they were great times and great people. I enjoyed every moment of it.

As the afternoon wore on, George reflected on various aspects of yesteryear life in the Inver area. There were the aspects he had experienced himself and those that had been passed down from an earlier era. Topics recalled included an 'ice house', the making of oilskins, socialising whilst net-mending, and a fast-track yawl-rigging technique. Yes, I was assured that is possible to rig a yawl in less than a minute, and that I would later see how it can be done!

While the 'ice house' phenomenon is well known, I was nonetheless surprised to learn that one existed on an estate in the Inver area. Ice was taken from a nearby river in the depths of winter and packed into a manmade underground chamber. There, using straw as an insulating material, it remained frozen for many months. Come summertime, when sprat fishing was in full swing, out came the ice to serve the all-important purpose of preserving the fish while on its way to market. Clearly, where there's a will there's a way.

George went on to talk about how oilskins were made. While again the technique he described is not unique, it's interesting to note that it was common practice in the local area. The depression years of the 1930s created a culture of repairing, reusing, making do, and not throwing things away, which lasted well into the 1950s. From then to the present day, a throw-away lifestyle associated with consumer society has held sway. It was in the reuse era at Inver that oilskins were fashioned from flour bag material. In the first instance, ladies experienced in fashioning garments from such fabric were called upon. Their job was to create a garment in the style of a fisherman's oilskin. With that part done, the article of clothing was painted with two or more coats of boiled linseed oil. Each coat was allowed to dry before the next was applied. The oilskin was then ready to wear.

One further point made by George on the importance of reuse and 'not throwing things away' highlighted how they would maximise the usefulness of the linseed oil. As each coat of oil was brushed on to the garment, a certain amount ran off. This was collected in a dish carefully positioned beneath the oilskin so it could be reused. It was very much a case of, waste not, want not.

When it came to socialising on a winter's night, George says, 'There was no better way of doing so than while mending cotton nets.' He went on to explain, 'When the fishing season ended, nets were cleaned, washed, dried and taken home. Then, during the long, dark nights, you would bring a bundle of net needing repair into the kitchen and set it down beside you. With an oil lamp providing light and the assistance of a hook screwed into the windowsill, you were ready to commence repair work. With the net supported by the hook, you sat in your chair and spread the yarn across your knees. You mended a section from the "top rope" to the "sole rope" and then moved the net on to the next section. At the same time you could socialise and have mighty craic with those who happened to drop in. It was a great way of passing a winter's night.'

So enthused was George about a locally used technique for raising and lowering sails on a yawl that he provided me with an actual demonstration. A boat resting on a trailer parked beside the house was used to demonstrate. Lying inside the boat was a mast-sized pole with a sail wrapped around it. The wrapped sail was held in place by three ropes (would-be stays) attached to the top of the pole and wound downwards. I was assured that, if necessary, the boat could be changed from a rowing boat to a sailing vessel, or vice versa, in one minute. I believed George; nevertheless, he set about proving his assertion. While I watched, he climbed aboard the boat and with dexterity that belied his years I witnessed the rigged boat materialise before my eyes. Incredibly, it had indeed been completed within one minute, as predicted.

He went on to explain that, naturally, the addition of sails greatly increased the speed at which boats travelled through water, and of course they reduced the need for laborious rowing. Nobody complained about that. 'It was,' George says, 'a good way of getting from A to B when the wind was favourable.' He remembers sails being used a great deal during driftnet herring seasons, when going out to the St John's Point area. Well, it is said that necessity is the mother of invention and maybe that was the case in this imaginative and speedy method of rigging a boat.

Back inside the house, with the sail-setting demonstration over, we moved on to discuss other aspects of George's life. Previous to my visit, I was informed that he had been a recipient of a Donegal Rehab 'People of the Year' Award in 2006. I checked the criterion of the award and read that, 'Those Donegal County Council-sponsored Awards recognise the enormous contributions made by citizens of the County to all areas of life. They are awarded to those who have touched lives and have made a difference. It is a way of giving people the recognition they deserve.' Well, I thought, I had better make independent enquires into what exactly George's forte was, or maybe there were many. The latter proved to be the case. I was told that he is a man of many parts. It is believed in his local community that, regardless of the cause, when he came on board, he more than pulled his weight. Perhaps it is for his fervent support of small fishing communities that he is best known. He has represented the case of inshore fishermen with passionate dignity at a local and national level. He is variously described as one who knows the local community and its needs, as a voice that is not afraid to speak out, as a man for all committees, as a friend to all, and as one for whom nothing is too much bother. In recent years he was the driving force behind the erection of a beautiful memorial stone at Ardaghey Graveyard, Inver. When I raised the People of the Year Award with George and asked how the honour came to be bestowed on him, the reply I received was, 'Well, I suppose I was involved in most community initiatives that have taken place over the years. I enjoyed helping out and doing things regardless, of the cause. There were local people who believed that I should allow my name to go forward. With a view to procuring letters of support for the bid, an organising group made contact with individuals and organisations that had known me over the years. The response was indeed tremendous. As they say, the rest is history.'

With the sun setting in the west, the time had come for me to set out on my homeward journey. Just as was I about to depart, George suggested I should visit the site of the recently erected memorial stone adjacent to Ardaghey Graveyard. There, enhanced by the late evening sunlight, stood a sculptured Wicklow granite stone creation, impressively designed and erected by local man Gary McHugh. Inscribed on it are the names of thirty-five people who lost their lives by drowning in the parish of Inver between 1830 and 1999. It was formally unveiled on 7 November 2004. Among the names listed are those of George's grandfather Peter Kennedy, and Peter's son Patrick, both of whom perished in 1904 as a result of an Inver Bay fishing-boat tragedy. In all, seven men perished in the incident. More recently, the neighbouring Inver Port families of Meehan and Kennedy have grieved over loved ones who were lost in the same area. In July 1995, uncle and nephew Charles and Stephen Meehan became victims. Twelve years later, in December 2007, it was the sad loss of father and son, Liam and Conor Kennedy, that once again caused family and local inhabitants to grieve. Both men died from the effects of hypothermia several hours after being rescued by helicopter.

Not only is the memorial stone a poignant reminder of the thirty-five people who have lost their lives, it is also testimony to the man who called a meeting on 8 December, 2003, at which a small committee was formed to look into the possibility of erecting such a monument. That man was George Gallagher.

8
RESOLUTE BELIEFS
Brian Crummy of Dún Laoghaire/Dunmore East

At the port of Dunmore East, County Waterford, I met up with well-known retired fisherman, skipper and boat owner, Brian Crummy. Brian, who originally hails from Dún Laoghaire, is now a long-time resident of Dunmore East. Brian is very much his own man. He is a man of resolute beliefs, which he steadfastly defends. There are few better placed to comment on the qualities of this skipper than those who fished on his boats. One such person who crewed on his boat *Lochtuddy* summed up Brian with the words, 'A real pro, always had new ideas.' Another man, who fished on Brian's 63ft *Nordcap*, said, 'He was a very particular man, and as honest a skipper owner as one could ask for. The boat was kept like a yacht.'

During our chat, Brian occasionally surprised me by holding what might be described as a minority view, but he backed up in his beliefs with laudable reasoning. As an example, he makes a very strong case for a method of fishing that is not universally well received – gillnetting. There is, he said, 'no problem with actual gillnetting; it is the greed of man that causes the problems. It is a very selective form of fishing and it should be encouraged.' He recalled gillnetting for hake using nets with the standard-size mesh and for some time couldn't understand why catches by his boat were poor in comparison to others. 'What I failed to realise,' he said, 'was that other boats were more successful because they were using nets with lesser than standard size mesh. They were, in fact, catching much smaller fish. It completely defeated the idea of stock conservation and is a horrible practice, driven by greed.'

When I suggested that some foreign boats had the reputation of being negligent with the use of gillnets, he laughed and said, 'There are not many foreign boats gillnetting now. The Irishman is doing as much harm, if not more, than foreign boats.' When I suggested that surely lost gill nets continue to fish indefinitely, Brian said, 'No, they don't. The view that they do so is ridiculous. With tides and other disturbances, nets quickly get balled up on the bottom. They become a tangled mass and they don't fish. You'll find that when lost gear is recovered: it's fouled up tight and has obviously not fished for some time. That is true regardless of majority opinion to the contrary.'

Another strongly held view, which again highlights the greed of man, relates to boats, which were built on applications for quotas to fish off the west coast, but ended up fishing off the African coast. They are, he says, 'doing more harm there than the Spanish or French boats are reputed to have done here.'

Brian began his association with the sea when as a young man, a boy even, he 'messed around' in small boats at Dún Laoghaire. In time, he followed his brother and fished out of Milford Haven. His stay was short. Word filtered through of lucrative herring fishing at Dunmore East:

We were working for buttons over there. We were told that you could make as much in a couple of months at Dunmore East as we were making for a whole year. So I came home and initially got a berth on the Arklow boat, *Pride of Ulster* (D362). I subsequently moved to Bill Cleary's *Glendalough* (D310), one of the highly rated pair of herring ringers to come off the slipway of Tyrrell's Boatyard, Arklow, in 1957. The other half of the duo, the *Glenmalure* (D147), was identical in all respects. The detail and thought put into the planning and design of those boats by Jack Tyrrell for the specific purpose of herring ringing is exemplified by the fact that they were literally flat-sided, to facilitate coming alongside one another.

By the early 1960s, Brian was in a position to consider getting his own boat. He, somewhat reluctantly, settled for the BIM 56-footer *Ard Ailbhe* (D198). The following is his memory of how it came about:

At the time I got her, in 1961, she was actually assigned to someone else but BIM offered her to me. I really wanted to buy a second-hand Scotch boat, a number of which were for sale at knockdown prices at the time. It was a situation that came about as result of a religious quandary that left boats on the west coast of Scotland without crews. However, attempts by Irish fishermen to finance the purchasing of those boats ran into difficulties. High interest rates on bank loans in comparison to those on deposits for newly built BIM boats were bordering on the prohibitive. Because of a significant horsepower difference between engines fitted in Scotch boats and those in BIM boats, generally 152hp as opposed to 114hp, the Scotch boats were a more attractive proposition in terms of fish-catching potential. There are various conclusions to be drawn regarding the large discrepancies in interest rates; for instance, could it have been

politically motivated and linked with a ply to keep BIM
boatyards in business?

Regardless of the reasons, Brian still resents the disproportion-
ate interest rate that prevented him from buying a Scotch boat
with greater fish-catching potential at less than half the price
he paid for the *Ard Ailbhe*.

He has a few other bones of contention regarding BIM at
that time. One is that he believes the cost of boats to the fishermen was artificially high; it was claimed by Jack Tyrrell that
he could build and sell boats at a much lower cost than the
BIM asking price, but he was 'advised' by the powers that be
not to do so. In fact, he was told that he wouldn't sell his boats
because BIM held the purse strings.

Further points with which Brian took issue where BIM
was concerned were that, having paid close to £20,000 for the
boat, he wasn't allowed to choose either its name or colour.
Regarding the name, he was obliged to select from one of
three, each beginning with the word *Ard*. There were also the
problems of boats built at BIM boatyards coming out at well
beyond the original cost, and late on delivery. Accumulated
problems along those lines eventually led to Irish fishermen
looking abroad to have their boats built at yards where an
agreed original cost stood and the delivery date was respected.
Naturally, that didn't go down well with established boatyards
at home. Brian believes it is no accident that several among
those who went on to become Ireland's most successful fishermen did not set out on the journey as BIM boat owners. In
hindsight, he believes that in the long term the advantages of
buying a more powerful-engined boat, even with the higher
rate of interest on loans, outstripped the BIM option. By the
mid-1960s Brian was in a position to look around for a boat
more in keeping with his original preference. He homed in on
the 63ft *Nordkap*, a Norwegian-built vessel fitted with a 230hp
engine. He successfully fished her for a number of years.

The 63ft Norwegian-built *Nordkap* (D119) in the 1960s.

In later years, at a time when whitefish stocks were running down, BIM began to encourage fishermen to diversify by looking towards alternative types of fishing. Brian, along with his working partner, took the bull by the horns and decided to have a go at razor-clam fishing, which was then in its infancy. He explained:

We sold the licence off the current boat, and invested the money in another boat, the *Trudella*, which we fitted out for razor fishing. Poor returns locally led us to fishing up the east coast, working off Howth, Skerries and Balbriggan. We were averaging landings of half to three-quarters of a ton per day. Encouraged by the return, we progressed from the single boat to a second, the *Osprey*, and finally to a third, the Killybegs-built, 65ft *Lora Don*. The three boats were landing into Wrights of Howth. As so often happens with fishing, all went well for a number of years, then the market more or less collapsed – though I understand it has picked up again in recent times. At any rate, a point was reached when we were not getting enough money to make it pay. The boats were tied up and eventually sold for scrap – except for the *Trudella*; she was purchased and converted to a pleasure craft.

Brian's direct link with fishing more or less came to a close around 2003, when a boat named *Wilhelmina S*, owned by him and his partner, was badly damaged when a fire broke out at sea. She was towed into port and subsequently sold on to a buyer in Norway.

It was unlikely that a man who holds strong opinions on the pros and cons of the Irish fish industry would stand idly by whenever a just cause raised its head. As such, it was not surprising that Brian became involved with the newly formed Irish Fishermen's Organisation (IFO) in the early 1970s, and later served as chairman. There was, at that time, he said, 'a general consensus among fishermen that a voice from the heart of the industry was needed to publicly air grievances'. Therefore, a call went out for the creation of an authoritative organisation to co-ordinate and maximise the lobbying power of commercial fishermen at both national and EC levels. Under the stewardship of general secretary Frank Doyle and chairman Kieran O'Driscoll, the IFO became a reality. The activities of the organisation led to our national government, the EC, and the media, taking heed of the difficulties Irish fishermen of the day were experiencing. Perhaps it was the potency of having such an organisation behind them that prompted fishermen to gather in Dublin and hold a rally at Leinster House in 1975. However, the formation of the Irish Fish Producers' Organisation (IFPO), an independent body set up in accordance with requirements laid down by national governments and the EC in the late 1970s, somewhat undermined the original effectiveness of the IFO. An element of uncertainty about which organisation best met their requirements left fishermen in a sort of limbo: should they follow one organisation or both? Significantly, the IFPO, with BIM's Mr James O'Connor, as chief executive, was funded partly by Brussels and partly by the state, whereas the IFO was wholly financially dependent on its members. There was no longer a level playing field. Obviously a lot of what went on in those distant days is now history. The world of producer organisations, co-operatives and indeed a revitalised IFO are another story.

A final point Brian made was that the late Frank Doyle, general secretary of the IFO, did not receive due recognition for his efforts in furthering the cause of Irish fishermen:

> The extent of the work Frank did behind the scenes went largely unnoticed. He was exceptional on the bureaucratic side of things and had a great talent for deciphering rules and regulations. He also excelled at documentation and taking on officials, be it Brussels or government personnel.

We could have gone on chatting much longer, had it not been for the fact that Brian had a pressing appointment. He had earlier suggested that I should meet his wife, Frances, before I left. As I bid Brian adieu, the good lady had still not returned from work. However, I had already heard enough to know she was not one to stand idly by, as is exemplified by the fact that she became the first female to join an all-weather RNLI lifeboat. Yes, in 1981 she became a crew member at Dunmore East Lifeboat Station. Subsequently, Frances, a member of the local, eminent Glody fishing family, participated in hundreds of call-outs. She retired after twenty years of service and received an award recognising her as the only woman in both Ireland and England to hold this service record. Well done to Frances!

9

BORN IN A LIGHTHOUSE

Ted Sweeney of Blacksod/Belmullet, County Mayo

Ted, a native of Blacksod, County Mayo, is yet another man I met on my travels. However, it was not in Blacksod we met, but at his now long-time Belmullet family home overlooking the expansive and aptly named Broadhaven Bay. As we conversed, chitchat at first, it soon became clear that he had extensive and interesting maritime experiences to share. I loved the sound of it all.

As we settled down to our serious chat, Ted's opening line was, 'I suppose it all began for me in 1947 when I was born in a lighthouse.' The lighthouse in question is that at Blacksod Point, situated at the southern end of the Erris peninsula, County Mayo. Erected in 1866, the granite building, with its white conical lantern at the top, is one of only two lighthouses world-wide of square-block construction. It was there that Ted's father, Ted Sr, served as attendant lighthouse keeper over a forty-eight-year period, extending from 1933 until his retirement in 1981.

Apparently a book could have been written on his experiences in the lighthouse service – not least, the now well-publicised part he played in the Second World War Normandy landings.

From 1969 to 1972, part of the Blacksod Lighthouse experienced what must have been a singular distinction for any lighthouse: it served as the local post office, with Ted Sr. acting as post master. It was in the headlines again in 1969, when it acted as the arrival point of Tom McClean, the first man to row a boat solo across the Atlantic Ocean. In 1991, it was almost destroyed in the infamous storm of that year. However, it survived and still stands proudly.

Steeped in a maritime background, young Ted grew up swimming and playing with his toy boats on the shoreline adjacent to Blacksod Lighthouse. His early memories are of many boats fishing out of Blacksod, and in particular, for a short period, the landing of sharks by a New Zealand native who had taken up residence locally.

Ted Sweeney in the grounds of his Belmullet home, with Broadhaven Bay in the background.

With his national school days behind him, Ted attended technical college. His career ambition was entirely focused on seagoing. Summer holidays were spent fishing out of Blacksod on the BIM 50-footer *Ros Donn*, owned and skippered by Paddy McShane of Teelin, County Donegal. During his time at technical college, he applied for an engineering cadetship with Irish Shipping Ltd, a company set up in 1941 to ensure Ireland could import and export essential goods during the Second World War. Success in his cadetship application led to his studying at the Crawford Municipal Technical Institute, Cork, and to appropriate experience at sea. In 1966, he joined Irish Shipping Ltd as a fully fledged marine engineer. He was to spend the following ten years traversing the oceans of the world on the company's ships. Extensive trading involved shipping between Canada and the USA to Japan, then back to Europe and down to Australia.

Ted married in 1972 and, with his wife Rita now accompanying him on occasional trips, the couple enjoyed visiting many exotic ports around the world. In those years, when general cargo ships were in use, it was customary to spend three or four days, sometimes more, in port. With the arrival of bulk carriers in later years, there was little or no time to go ashore; turnabout became almost immediate. I was greatly surprised at the number of Irish Shipping vessels Ted had sailed on. After starting out on the *Irish Oak*, over the years he was to spend time on each of the following: *Irish Alder*, *Irish Spruce*, *Irish Pine*, *Irish Cedar*, *Irish Plane*, *Irish Star*, *Irish Elm* and *Irish Larch*.

When I asked Ted if he recalled any particular highlights from his deep-sea years with Irish Shipping, he immediately referred to his encounters with Soviet Union seamen. He found that, in contrast to the image of 'Russians' imparted to him during his school days, he found them to be most helpful and terrific people. He went on to say:

Blacksod Lighthouse. (Courtesy of Seamus Mayock)

In those days, pre-break-up of the Soviet Union, their general cargo ships were similar to ours in that they carried around forty crew members. However, they differed greatly in one respect – each boasted a fully equipped operating theatre and an onboard doctor. Accidents do happen at sea and crew members get injured. When such incidents occurred, maybe out in the middle of the Pacific Ocean, and we called for assistance, 99 per cent of the time it was a 'Russian ship' that answered offering help, and diverting to do so. The fact that they carried doctors when we didn't was something that fascinated us. The explanation is based to a large extent on the education system then practised in the Soviet Union; it was very good, it was free, and open to all, right through to third level. Some students opted to become doctors. As with other graduates, there was a price to pay: the government demanded that in return for a free education, individuals should serve a specified number of years in state service. Among the choices were the army, navy, merchant navy, or to spend time at a Siberian outpost. Not surprisingly, the majority of doctors choose the merchant navy as it provided an opportunity to experience many parts of the world.

Ted was also taken by the fact that safety considerations on Soviet ships were well ahead of those on ships hailing from other countries. He cited totally enclosed lifeboats as an example – 'It was,' he said, 'years and years later before our ships had enclosed lifeboats.'

I asked Ted about the demise of Irish Shipping Ltd. What happened to the company that for years carried the brand of, 'Small but Great'? Where did it all go wrong? In 1981, all seemed well when the company placed an order for a new 75,000dwt bulk panamax carrier at Verolme Dockyard, Cork; yet the company was liquidated in November 1984. Ted explained:

The demise is yet another casualty brought about by lack of expertise in maritime affairs on the part of successive Irish governments. Irish Shipping Ltd was doing fine! After the Second World War, it traded on and was a very successful company. During the first oil crisis [1973] coal became a great cargo, so Irish Shipping diverted into that. They did likewise in the second oil crisis [1979]. All was going well up to that stage – money was certainly being made. However, there was a serious weakness at top-management level, brought about by the granting of directorships to friends and relations of politicians who knew more about matters relating to land and animals than to commercial shipping. A serious blunder, made when working with an English company [Reardon Smith Line] during the second oil crisis, was to prove catastrophic. When Irish Shipping hadn't sufficient ships to transport coal, they began chartering in vessels, mainly of Chinese ownership. They did so for up to nine-year periods, periods when a maximum of six to twelve months would have been the normal undertaking for more experienced shipping directors. It was preposterous! Shipping trade can change very quickly.

I asked how and why such erroneous decisions came about.

> It happened because Irish Shipping directors of the day didn't
> know any better. The crews knew it was crazy but their opin-
> ions were dismissed. The real crunch came when the oil crises
> passed and coal was no longer a big-time cargo commodity;
> chartered ships were soon idle while the company was stuck
> with paying hefty charter fees. Irish Shipping was brought
> to its knees; its financial lifeblood drained away because of
> outrageous decision-making. In 1984 the Irish government
> liquidated the company, leaving trained seamen, deck officers
> and engineers to set about finding shore jobs. It was a disaster.

Ted was not a casualty of the Irish Shipping downfall because
he had severed links with the company in 1976. Instead of
high-seas tripping, he embarked on work closer to home; he
joined Irish Lights and remained in the lighthouse service
until the year 2000. During that time, he served as engineer on
the tenders *Atlanta* and *Gray Seal*. He recalls that period of his
seagoing as, 'a pleasant time that gave him a great knowledge
of the Irish coast'. He added, 'We called at every nook and
cranny.' The Philips & Son Ltd-built 65m *Atlanta* (1959) was
modernised and lengthened by 5.3m in 1975, resulting in an
overall length of 70.3m and an increase in gross tonnage from
1,185.18 to 1,300. When sold to Greek-based owners in 1988
and renamed *Taris*, she was converted to a luxury yacht.

In 2000, when the new *Granuaile* (the third vessel in the
Irish Lighthouse Service so named) came into service, Ted
opted for redundancy. He smiled as he reflected on an incident he recalled from his time on one of the Irish Lights ships.
It occurred in the days when driftnet salmon fishing around
the coast was in its heyday, and relations between Irish naval
vessels' personnel and fishermen were far from amicable. The
incident in question is remembered by Ted as follows:

Gray Seal at Dun Laoghaire. (Author's collection)

We were coming around the north Donegal coast, off Malin Head, during the salmon-fishing season. Our ships were readily recognisable by fishermen and presented no problems for them. As such, we were politely advised over the radio by 'blue boat', 'red boat' or whatever [no names given] that nets were shot in this direction or that, and would we alter course a little in order to avoid them. At the same time, one of the navy vessels on salmon-fishing patrol arrived on the scene. Addressing one of the fishing boats, a call came over the radio from the patrol ship, boldly identifying itself as 'the warship *Graine*'. We listened with interest to hear what the response would be. There was no reply for several minutes, then over the airwaves in a distinctive Donegal accent came three words, 'warship my bollocks'. There was no further mention of 'warship' after that.

Ted's days with Irish Shipping and Irish Lights may have been behind him, but his seagoing days were far from over. For the better part of the three years following his departure from Irish Lights, he became an employee of P&O Cross Channel Ferries. During those years, he served as chief engineer on ferry ships operating the Larne–Cairnryan route. It was, he said, 'hard going. After a fortnight on the ferries you were glad to get a fortnight off. You were on duty twelve hours a day. It was like a bus service – over and back, back and over. After a few days you didn't really know whether you were coming or going. You just did the job, got off after two weeks, went home, recharged and then away again. It was nevertheless a secure job and I made some great friends and met great people while on the ferries – not least Union Hall man Gerard Burns.'

When an offer of employment came to Ted from the Marine Institute (*Foras Na Mara*), he made the engineer superintendant of P&O Ferries aware of his intention to leave. The response was, 'You have a go at it and if you are not happy your job will be waiting here for you.'

'I thought that was very fair indeed,' said Ted. Of course it was fair, but it speaks volumes for the regard in which Ted was held by his employers.

His move from P&O Ferries took him on into a completely new phase in seagoing activity. In 2002, while the state-of-the-art research vessel *Celtic Explorer* (see Marine Institute website for details) was at the building stage in the Damem Shipyards, Holland, Ted was approached and asked if he would be interested in joining the crew of the 2,425-ton vessel. 'The decision,' he says, 'was an easy one to make.' The general-purpose research vessel was splendidly equipped to carry out exploration and scientific study of the ocean and its phenomena. She is owned and operated by the Marine Institute, Ireland's national agency for marine research. The *Celtic Explorer* is the Marine Institute's national platform for offshore research activities, including extensive fisheries research, a topic in which Ted has a deep interest.

Celtic Explorer on the high seas.

Having been present throughout the build phase at the Damen Shipyard, Ted's intimate knowledge of all the engineering aspects involved later proved to be an invaluable asset to his employers. As chief engineer, he oversaw the operation and maintenance of all machinery on the 65.5m research vessel – a significant undertaking on the €30 million ship that on occasion remained at sea for up to a month at a time, and accommodated thirty-five personnel, including about twenty scientists.

When Ted began to talk about the *Celtic Explorer* and his experiences on the ship, he clearly became more enthused than he had hitherto been. His opening words were:

> I enjoyed being on the *Celtic Explorer* so much; every day was different, it was totally different to any other seafaring I had done. I realised that I had kept the best ship until last. I've been at sea all my life in all sorts of ships – cargo ships, lighthouse tenders and car ferries – but none of them compared to my experiences on the *Celtic Explorer*.

So what was it that created such an impression?

> We were doing everything from fishing to oceanography, to weather research, to seabed mapping, and expeditions involving the remotely operated deepwater vehicle (ROV). The ROV is fitted with numerous cameras and sample-taking arms. The monitored observations were fascinating, even though half the time you were only seeing seabed. Yet, you were afraid to take your eyes off the screen in case you missed something. It was a funny sensation that you were looking at something no one else had ever seen. Occasionally a big inquisitive fish showed up. We used it in deep canyons west of the Porcupine Banks while researching fresh coral, and for taking samples of sponges and other materials from the Irish Continental Shelf at a depth of almost 3,000 metres. The last time I used it we were down off the Azores.

During Ted's years on the *Celtic Explorer*, she traversed the oceans in order to make various aspects of underwater research possible. She sailed to the Caribbean in 2008, where researchers carried out fish surveys on behalf of the United Nations. At another stage, working in the Denmark Strait, research scientists from the British Geological Institute studied fresh lava from underwater volcanoes in rocks dredged up by the *Celtic Explorer*.

Fisheries research carried out by *Celtic Explorer* scientists is, of course, of great interest to those involved in harvesting the seas around our shores. I asked Ted to enlighten me a little on the matter:

> Some trips were dedicated exclusively to fishing – trawling mainly. It had to be done to a protocol. We trawled the exact same ground in daylight year after year, using nets of the same specifications for exactly the same length of time – ½-hour tows. That was done in order to compare like with like. The

main interest was in juvenile fish. Scientists aboard measured and checked ages of all species landed. From their findings, predictions were made regarding future stocks. Present stocks were of little interest. The focus was on the likely state of future stocks. The information accrued by the scientists was used as the basis for drawing up fishing quota levels for subsequent years. Occasionally we did comparative tows with Spanish or British research vessels and later compared results. The comparisons made afforded indications as to the state of future stocks. In carrying out pelagic surveys, blue whiting, etc., an area from, say, west of Kerry maybe up to the Faroe Islands would be divided between ourselves, Norwegians, Dutch, Scottish and occasionally Russian research ships. Information coming from each vessel was pooled and later used in defining quotas. In the cases of north-west and south-west herring fisheries, we carried out solo surveys, with some information also coming from commercial fishing boats. A lot of that work was done through acoustic echo sounding, working along lines in a grid. It is imperative that a grid system is employed and that lines are followed. Occasionally a trawl was shot to pick up samples to ensure that sounder markings were that of herring rather than another species. Commercial fishing vessel skippers sometimes disagree with our findings but in order to carry out surveys one has to work within the confines of the particular system in place.

In October 2012, having completed ten years' service as chief engineer on the *Celtic Explorer*, Ted retired. Remarks made at the time by Bill Dwyer, contract manager at P&O Maritime Ireland, gives an indication of the regard in which Ted was held – 'Ted played a prominent part in creating the world-class reputation that the vessel now has and for that we are very grateful.'

Ted holds strong views on the mismanagement of maritime affairs by successive Irish governments. 'Very poorly handled,' he says. His belief is that, since its establishment by the state, it has been steadfastly ruled and influenced by personnel from the agricultural sector and the clergy. Although he is not anti-farming, he believes, 'the civil service to have been massively oversubscribed by people coming from farming backgrounds'. He also believes, 'the Church virtually controlled the education system for far too long'. The mix of state and Church either failed to comprehend or chose to ignore the riches that abound in the waters surrounding this island nation. As Ted rightly says, in our schools we were told, and indeed it was drummed into us, 'that agriculture was Ireland's natural resource'. That was the mantra. Ignorance of the sea and its enormous worth by the vast majority of those who have had an input into the running of the country has had dire consequences. In the domain of maritime affairs, dreadful decisions have been made. Ted referred to the inexplicable undertakings that led to the demise of Irish Shipping. Previous to that fiasco, ill-conceived negotiations in return for comparatively small rewards led to our government feebly handing over the majority of our offshore fisheries to foreign fleets. Currently, it seems that the majority of wealth derived from the considerable offshore gas and oil fields will find its way into the coffers of foreign conglomerates. Yes, there are extreme costs involved in the exploration and development of the fields, and it is also true that the business is risky and that a serious amount of money could be lost. On the other hand, the rewards are big if all goes well. The point is that without investigating other avenues of dealing with *our* offshore oil and gas exploration (e.g. the Norwegian model), or indeed consulting some of the many Irish people working in oil exploration abroad, civil servants at home have gone ahead and unilaterally made decisions. Consequently, the possibility of this country getting a fair return is now remote.

As we sat looking out over the shimmering waters of Broadhaven Bay, Ted reflected on the camaraderie that existed among seagoing folk. On a personal note, he recalled that in his forty-seven years at sea, he could count the number of people he didn't get on with using the fingers of one hand; he held up three. He went on to say:

> It says a lot for the many, many people I met. We all depended on each other and helped each other out. Most of the crew on the *Celtic Explorer* were ex-fishermen. I found them to be terrific people. On some of the deep sea ships, occasionally an element of demarcation syndrome did surface. You never got that from ex-fishermen; anything they could do, they did, and cared for ships very well without having to be told. I still keep in touch with men from years and years ago. The sea was very good to me; I made a good living and enjoyed it.

Having spent an entire afternoon chatting with Ted's at his Tallagh Hill home in Belmullet, I left feeling that a great story of a lifetime at sea had unfolded in an enlightening and most eloquent manner – a story that had to be put on paper!

10

DIED JUST OVER A YEAR AGO

Marion, Andy and John of North Donegal

Some years ago, at the Galway Skipper Expo, I fell into conversation with a fisherman from Port-na-Blagh, County Donegal. He suggested that I should have a chat with Sammy Scott, a man then resident at Downings. Sammy, he said, will tell you all about yesteryear fishing in the Port-na-Blagh and Downings area of County Donegal. Somehow I didn't get around to making contact until over a year later. Having dialled the phone number I had been given, a lady identifying herself as Marion answered. I asked if it was possible to speak with Sammy. Her response was, 'Sammy died just over a year ago.' Having expressed my deepest sympathy, and having explained the reason for my call, it became clear that Marion was au fait with much of Sammy's fishing career. As our conversation progressed, I asked if she would mind if I called on her if I were in the Downings area sometime. Marion replied, 'That would be no problem. I'd be delighted, just let me know in advance.'

Some months later, I did visit. To add to her own memories of Sammy's experiences, Marion had arranged for me to meet two Dunfanaghy gentlemen, Andy Hanlon and John Parry, both of whom had been well acquainted with Sammy during his lifetime, and with his seagoing fishing activities.

As Marion spoke, it quickly became clear that Sammy had possessed an entrepreneurial spark and in some ways appeared to be somewhat ahead of his time. He was passionate and single-minded about whatever he became involved in. As a young man with a farming background, he left the parental home in Inishowen to work in London. With money saved, he returned to County Donegal and set up a business involving a gravel pit, coupled with related machinery and plant hire. By then (the early 1970s), he would have been in his late twenties or early thirties. Sammy worked very hard to make the business a success, but had recurring difficulties collecting payment from clients, which proved both demoralising and costly. So what was to be done?

Andy Hanlon and John Parry.

A chance trip to Burtonport changed everything. John Parry recalled how Sammy became involved in fishing as follows:

> He accompanied a fisherman friend, Val Robinson, on a trip to Burtonport, where Val sold lobsters to a merchant. With the consignment of lobsters handed over, Val immediately received payment for the delivery. Observing the transaction, Sammy reflected on his business with many debtors from whom payment was not forthcoming. There had to be a better way and maybe this was it. He would look into the possibility of making a career move to fishing.

As was his way, he wasted little time. Listening carefully to the snippets of information coming from Andy and John, the story of Sammy's fishing days gradually emerged. To begin with, he got a berth on a boat named *Sea Flower* and fished on her for some time before purchasing the *Yvonne*, a decked cruiser stern boat of 32–35ft in length. Having got a taste for fishing, and having found it more lucrative than plant hire, etc., he decided to buy a bigger boat, the 50ft BIM-built *Ros Droichead*, previously owned by John Canning, Greencastle. He fished her out of Port-na-Blagh. Seining was the current form of fishing and to hone his skills in the art, Bert Robinson (brother of Val and owner of the BIM 50-footer *Ros Beag*), went to sea with Sammy. A passing remark was made by Andy, 'Bert did his best but it was hard to tell Sammy anything.'

In the years that followed, Sammy continued to fish successfully. Marion remarked, 'There were loads of haddock and all that kind of fish to be caught then.' All was going well until disaster struck. On a night of strong westerly wind and ferocious hail showers, the *Ros Droichead* broke away from her moorings, ran aground, and she suffered irreparable damage that included of a broken keel. The best efforts of Andy, John and others failed to save the Baltimore-built BIM 50-footer.

It was a sad end for the beautiful, varnished-hulled boat I personally witnessed coming down the slipway on a bright and sunny day in January 1954.

As a replacement for the *Ros Droichead*, Sammy rented the 60ft Tyrrell-built *Muiranna* from James McCloud at Killybegs. Subsequently Andy fished on her with Sammy out of Port-na-Blagh, Killybegs and Rathmullan. Sadly, the *Muiranna*, once amongst the elite of the Killybegs fleet and certainly James McCloud's pride and joy, ended her days as a burnt-out wreck.

Sammy's next venture involved salvaging a boat: the 56ft Scotch-built *Summer Rose*. She was lying at Buncrana Pier in very poor condition, so poor that the sea had free passage in and out of her as the tide came and went. A wreck for all intent and purposes, but, as Andy remarked, 'Sammy would try anything'. Marion too mentioned that, 'Sammy liked doing that kind of thing, taking on a challenge'. Andy recalled the sequence of events involving the *Summer Rose*:

> She was accidentally but extensively holed at Buncrana pier, so much so that there was no simple or inexpensive way of dealing with the damage. Moving the boat away from the pier was, or appeared to be, a total nonstarter. When all seemed lost Sammy went and purchased her for little or nothing. Somehow, by unconventional and complicated means, he succeeded in carrying out a repair job that partially sealed the leaks. His plan was to take her across Lough Swilly to Alan Stewart's boatyard at Ramelton. With a Browne family boat from Inch Island secured to carry out the tow, Sammy hired three pumps to ensure the *Summer Rose* didn't sink on passage. The crossing was made successfully. At the boatyard, wide-ranging work was carried out on vessel and engine. Against all odds, Sammy's determination ensured that what

had been a partially sunken, derelict wreck at Buncrana pier returned to seining out of Port-na-Blagh during the week, and taking angling parties out at weekends.

Later, Sammy moved base from Port-na-Blagh to Downings, where he continued to fish. While there, the *Summer Rose* was again to become the victim of a leakage problem. Moored off Downings Pier, a series of malfunctions involving batteries and pumps led to the boat sinking. With huge difficulty she was re-floated. 'She was badly shaken,' Andy recalled. Undaunted, with relentless pumping Sammy had her towed to Mevagh, where he spent a winter getting her into ship shape to go back fishing. Shaking his head and smiling, Andy added, 'He was some survivor, a character, a man of many talents, and any "head case" that ever came to the locality ended up fishing with him.' What a pity, I thought, that I had not met up with Sammy!

As he advanced in years, he found that fishing was no longer what it used to be – fish became scarce and crews were no longer so readily available, or indeed so dependable. He decided to decommission the *Summer Rose* and concentrated full-time on taking out angling parties. He quickly built up a considerable clientele base, hailing from far and near. As was his nature, he gave 100 per cent to whatever he became involved in. The angling business was no different. He began making up his own fishing gear and, to facilitate what became a very successful venture, he purchased a 36ft purpose-built fibreglass angling boat, which he named *Summer Rose*. However, his adventurous and never-say-die lifestyle received a serious setback when he was in his late sixties. The man who had been so fit and so energetic throughout his lifetime developed cancer and died aged 70 years.

The *Summer Rose*, Sammy's fibreglass angler.

Reflecting on Sammy's ambition and 'try-anything flair' outside of fishing, mention was made firstly by Marion and later by Andy, of a steel lobster pot-making business he embarked upon. He based the operation at Horn Head. According to Andy, the manufacturing and marketing procedures were efficiently carried out: 'On Monday morning Sammy began by cutting steel rods to make 100 pots and by 12 o'clock on Saturday all 100 were made up. He sold and personally delivered any amount of the pots down along the Mayo coast. In time steel pots began to be imported from Scotland and that more or less put an end to Sammy's business.'

Another of Sammy's enterprising businesses recalled by Andy and John was the shipping coal and firewood blocks to Tory Island. He also transported occasional loads of sand to the island. He was, Andy said, 'held in very high regard in Tory.'

So what about the two men who had given up their afternoon to chat with me? Well, clearly they had been close to the
fishing scene in the Dunfanaghy/Port-na-Blagh and Downings
areas for several years from the 1960s onwards. In their time,
both men experienced whitefish trawling, salmon drift netting
and potting. Much of the discussion centred on the salmon-
fishing heyday. From the mid-1960s onwards, little-used
half-deckers were awakened from their slumbers to take part
in the bonanza. Not all owners had ready capital to invest in
nets; there were wealthy individuals who were willing to help
out, but there were strings attached. It was a case of, 'I'll pay for
nets but there will be an obligation to sell your fish through
me'. This was not always the most rewarding arrangement for
the fisherman. However, one way or another the amount of
salmon-season money generated was sufficient to entice men
back from Scotland and England. Andy recalled a particular
half-decker regularly landing 300 salmon for a night's fishing.
Practically all fish was sold through the Burtonport Fishermen's
Co-op, which was regarded as 'a very big outfit'. To give an idea
of the amount of salmon handled by the Co-op, John referred
to a passing remark by the manager on a particular day: 'There
was poor fishing here this morning – only 4,200 fish came in.'

As time went on, more and more boats joined the fleet. From
Greencastle alone, John said, 'there were fourteen trawlers
fishing salmon out of Downings in the mid-1970s'. Problems
associated with the use of monofilament nets, naval patrol
boats, a restriction on fishing outside a 6-mile limit and weekend fishing, began to arise. But that was not all. Difficulties
experienced by boats taking out angling parties, especially at
weekends, arose; negotiating a passage around lengthy nets
was, in some cases, taking up to an hour. It was a problem
that made newspaper headlines. Worse was still to come in
the form of 'big Atlantic seals'. Apparently the seals followed
large gillnetters inshore, where they plundered salmon from

nets of half-deckers and other smaller boats. Andy said, 'If you were out fishing and a gillnetter passed in you might as well go home.' John added, 'At the finish-up, if a salmon hit the net 10 yards away you wouldn't have a 15 per cent chance of getting it. The seals could still take the fish when the net was virtually aboard the boat. It was a case of all change from the early days when shot nets could be left and hauled later. Even a constant patrolling of nets wasn't enough as time went on.'

The afternoon was wearing on, but Andy and John, briefly joined by local journalist, Moses Alcorn, were happy to recall the goings-on of other days. The conversation moved on to lobster, crayfish and crab fishing. Something that is now forgotten, or not known by many people, is that in the 1950s, and maybe into the 1960s, lobsters were sold by the dozen, rather than by weight. It was not unknown for large ones to be thrown back into the sea in order to make more room for smaller ones in a box. Unbelievable quantities of shellfish were caught and transported to Burtonport, where purpose-built ponds owned by the Co-op were in place to receive them. Andy recalled witnessing seventy and eighty boxes of crayfish, caught in tangle nets, leaving the small port of Ballyness (near Falcarragh). There was, he said, 'as much money for them then as there is now – it was great money'.

Crabs, caught in nets and pots (creels), were also a lucrative source of income. Andy talked about catches from one small net producing enough toes (claws) to fill two boxes and recalled that anywhere a pot with fresh bait was shot in Sheephaven Bay, it was full to the top with large crabs in no time. He cited a landing of thirty-eight boxes from fifty pots. For half-deckers, 100 pots would have been a 'big fleet', 120 above average. For the most part, double 'fleets' were hauled per day; nowadays the number is likely to be in the 500 or more bracket. Some boats are said to be hauling 1,600 pots per day, reportedly with three per minute coming up.

I decided the time had come to part company with the three amiable persons who had ever so kindly chatted with me throughout the afternoon in the Andy's front room. I left enlightened, not only about the life and times of the late Sammy Scott, but also about the local fishing scene as they remembered it.

11

KERRY BLOOD IN THEIR VEINS

Pat Moore of Killybegs, County Donegal

It was a pleasant early spring morning in Killybegs. Boats waiting to unload thousands of tons of a variety of boarfish, commonly known as 'reds', were queued up at the pier. Across the way, at the Blackrock Pier, and further down the harbour at the new pier, several mackerel tank boats were tied up. Having fished their quotas in a two-month period, they would now have a long vacation. That's the way it works.

I had come to Killybegs to meet up with Pat Moore, a member of a prominent Killybegs fishing family. Martin Moore, Pat's father, pioneered the way for what could be described as a fishing family dynasty at the port. He arrived from Dingle, County Kerry, on the west Donegal coast in the early 1930s and was followed by his father Ned, and brothers Paddy, Benny, Mossie and Eddie. All of that took place years before Pat was born and so, beyond hearsay, he has no first-hand knowledge of happenings at that time. However, some years ago, during my discussions with visionary fisherman *par excellence*, the late James McLeod, he put in context the standing in which the Moore family was held. He spoke glowingly of the 'Kerry boats', and their owners, the Moore family, who came to Donegal in the 1930s. He said:

> They were trawling behind St John's Point even before we got the *Martha Helen* in 1936. Martin Moore was a particularly intelligent man and when he saw us seine netting he was determined to get into it. To that end, he purchased a boat named the *Mulroy Bay* that was lying up in Mevagh and had her re-engined. He was fortunate that his father, Ned, who fished with him, looked after the engine and, indeed, you could have taken your breakfast off the floor of the engine room so clean and tidy it was.

Pat Moore at his Killybegs home.

Pat understands that the same Ned, his grandfather, was originally a native of Fenit, County Kerry, and went on to say, 'Benny [Pat's uncle] maintained that Ned spent some of his early years in the Russia Navy.'

Throughout the decades from their arrival in the early 1930s to the present day, members of the Moore family were destined to fish multiple boats out of Killybegs. Among the vessels owned by various family members were the 48ft *Mulroy Bay*, the 56ft *Girl Eileen*, the 70ft *Magnificent*, the 70ft *Mulroy Bay II*, the 80ft *Aqua Marine*, the 50ft *Brothers Hope*, and the 56ft *Favourite*.

Pat began his fishing career at the age of 16, acquired a skipper's ticket along the way, and retired at 60. He learned his trade on boats owned and fished by his father and uncles. While he mainly fished off the Donegal coast, he was also involved in harvesting the seas down along the west coast. Sligo Bay, Killala Bay, Achill Island and Clew Bay figured prominently, with the Aran Islands and the far-off Porcupine Bank also featuring. When skippering Willie Gallagher's 75ft *Caranndon* (Tyrrell-built, 1972), he recalled landing very large catches of prawns at the Galway port of Rosaveal, and, on one occasion, boarding 200 boxes in one haul.

When I asked about his early memories of fishing out of Killybegs, this is what he had to say:

> Times were great then. I remember the pier in the spring of the year when you couldn't get moving with boxes of cod piled all over the place. Then you'd have the herring after that. So many boxes of fish! The buyers kept running out of empty boxes. Instead a row of barrels were put across the Co-op shed doorway into which we dumped the fish. Then a gang would come along and shovel salt into the barrels.

Laughing, he recalled that at one time a representative of a French company arrived to buy herring through local merchants. A barrelling business was set up in a disused coalyard, which still had quite a lot of the black stuff lying around. The word was that when the operation first got underway there was almost as much coal as salt being shovelled into the barrels. But, as Pat says in his best Killybegs accent, 'Sure, the herring were salted anyway.' Again he laughed aloud as another anecdote from those days came to mind. He went on to say:

> The Frenchman died whilst at Killybegs. When his employers were contacted as regards funeral arrangements they suggested it would be best if he were buried in Killybegs, but that arrangements should be made for return of his company car to France – no return of the body, but the car, yes. A case of getting priorities right.

On a more serious note, Pat reflected on the fact that a great cod fishery existed offshore at Killybegs in those days but over the years it disappeared completely. Various reasons have been given for its demise, such as pollution and the use of gillnets.

Throughout our chat, Pat talked a great deal of the years spent ringing and trawling down off the Sligo and Mayo coasts in the 1960s and early '70s. He referred to the very long trips from the tip of Achill all the way up Clew Bay to land catches at Westport, which took four hours or so, and to the unbelievable shoals of herring that packed into Sligo Bay, virtually right up to the bridge in the town, for a few seasons. As he talked on about those days, the following incident came to mind:

> I remember fishing in Sligo Bay on the *Magnificent*. We were towing for herring, using a bottom trawl with doors. The boat could carry up the 350 cran. She was Scotch-built and had previously been used by her owners for running 1,000 boxes of herring at a time from Northern Ireland ports to Scotland. Going back to my story, we were boarding around

120 cran each shot on one particular day. All was going well. We had hold-gear fitted so as to fill one side first, then the other, and finally the middle. All the while, the hatch boards were in place so that there was no human contact with what was going on below. The winch was forehead and belt-driven. We had no idea that anything was wrong until herring began to spew around the deck as they arrived from below, carried up by the winch belt. We quickly realised that the forehead bulkhead had given way. Talk about a mess, I'll never forget it. Fortunately the boat wasn't in any way unbalanced by the mishap.

Pat went on to state that the 56-footer *Girl Eileen* wasn't particularly good. He spoke of times when, coming from behind St John's Point (off Killybegs) well loaded with herring, when the sea used to come in through the hawse pipes and back along the deck. 'She used to be nearly like a submarine,' he said.

Girl Eileen – a model by Frankie Kennedy, Killybegs.

When I asked about close encounters of any kind he might have been involved in during his fishing career, he thought for a while before saying:

There was the night on the *Girl Eileen*. It was one of the years we were down in Achill, herring ringing. The three Moore family-owned boats were there. I was on the *Girl Eileen* with my Uncle Mossie, my father Martin was on the *Vigilant* and my Uncle Benny was on the *Brothers Hope*. One night as the weather deteriorated, the wind went around to the south-west. We decided to move south and take shelter behind Clare Island in the mouth of Clew Bay. We dropped anchor and, being happy that all was well, the crew of the *Girl Eileen* went below to play cards. There was a chap keeping an eye out in the wheelhouse but somehow he didn't notice that the wind changed around to the north. The anchor chain broke and the next thing we knew was the boat had been thrown onto rocks and lying on her side. Panic broke out! Being a good swimmer, I wasn't all that worried. Strange the things that enter your mind at times like that – I remembered that I had a ten-shilling note under the mattress and off I went down to the cabin to retrieve it. That was my priority! Some crew members struggled to remain upright as they slipped around on the sloping deck. Fortunately, in the midst of considerable consternation, a wave came along and somehow dislodged the boat from the reef. By that time the men in the other two boats were aware of our mishap and were standing by to help. As a precaution, the *Vigilant* came alongside and took some crew off the *Girl Eileen*. Mossie, I and one other chap stayed aboard. The boat was making water and needed constant pumping out. Mossie steered her up through the islands and on into Westport. From there we arranged for shipwrights to come from the Killybegs boatyard to assess the damage. It transpired that there was keel and planking damage but that temporary repair work could be carried out there and then. We continued to fish for a couple of weeks before returning home. Apparently the long trip back to Killybegs in the damaged boat didn't appeal to some crew members, who concocted reasons for travelling by other means.

Again Pat laughed as he recalled crew members jumping in trepidation from the *Girl Eileen* onto the *Vigilant*. He believes that if there had been long-jump Olympic gold medals on offer, they would have won hands down.

Pat was by now on a roll and incidents from his fishing experiences of yesteryear kept coming back. He went on to tell me an amusing tale from a time he was night trawling in Killala Bay:

> There was good fishing, plenty of flats. The problem was that locals had salmon nets anchored out. We had managed to keep clear of the nets. Nevertheless there was concern that their gear might get damaged. They struck on a novel idea to get me to stop fishing. They went off, spoke to the parish priest and asked him to approach me with their concerns. That he did! I pointed out to the reverend gentleman that I had to make a living too and suggested that the salmon men haul their nets and let me fish for a few nights. Nothing doing, the persuasive PP insisted that I move on. We came to the conclusion that those fellows, that gang with the salmon nets, would try anything in order to get their way. We used to laugh about it.

Around the time Pat and Bridgid married in 1965, he bought the 70ft *Magnificent* from his father, Martin, who replaced her with the 80ft *Aqua Marine*. The re-engined *Aqua Marine* was a fine boat but it was a bit too much for the ageing Martin. As Pat put it, 'He wasn't fit for her at that stage.' Pat decided to sell the *Magnificent* (to Pat Connelly of Connemara) and take the *Aqua Marine* off his father's hands. Pat found it difficult to make her pay her way and 'gave her back'. 'To be honest,' he said, 'it was a nightmare.'

During his extensive fishing career, Pat always did his 'own thing', so maybe it's not too surprising that in the late 1970s he was the first skipper to engage in weekend fishing out of Killybegs. It was a practice that did not immediately meet with universal approval. However, one year on, many others followed suit. He explained, 'It was wintertime, we were bottom-trawling close to home, an hour or so steaming, landing nightly, and fishing was good. I had a great crew who agreed that if we took Friday off, we could fish Saturday and Sunday. That way, we were "ahead of the game", even if days were lost during the week because of bad weather. It was a great start to have maybe up to 200 boxes of fish landed on Monday morning.'

Pat told me another story that deserves to be retold. In the late 1980s, he fished what was an 'old boat' for an acquaintance. As he put it:

There were plenty of bucks who wouldn't put their foot on her deck. Down in the engine room when she rolled, the oil tanks moved and even the engine moved – yes, the engine moved. There were two of us running her and there was also a young buck from Balbriggan on the crew. He was a little bit nervy and went on about safety. Not surprisingly, taking the condition of the boat into account, he kept asking for a life jacket. I don't know if he ever got one. One day we were out behind St John's Point. There was a good swell running. The young chap was down in the hold and from the wheelhouse I could see him beckoning me to come down. I put my head out the window and asked what was wrong. 'Come on down,' he says, 'I have something to show you.' Down I went and he pointed towards the side of the boat. There I could see that every time she rolled, gaps appeared in the planking, allowing St John's Point to be seen in the distance. In spite of all that, we were 'making a big fishing in her'; she was a great boat to tow. The first week out, for three days, we made £800 per man. In fact, the first trip we landed fifty-six boxes of brill, turbot and sole. We had the boat for two years and, to be honest, I made more money in her than I made in any boat.

During my visit to the Moore household, I met up with Pat's sons, Jason and Stevie. Both were currently fishing on the tank boat *Sheanne*, Jason as skipper and Stevie as deck crew. As with most boats engaged in mackerel fishing, she had very successfully fished her quota, and had just made a landing of 1,000 tons of boarfish at a Danish port. The two young men purchased the 56ft *Favourite* a few years back and fished her during that long, imposed summer break. However, a year later, with the expensive Code of Practice looming, they decided to sell her on.

So what of the Moore family members that made their way up from Kerry all those years ago? Well, all have passed on except for Benny, who retired to Dingle, where he still lives.

Pat Moore with sons Jason and Stevie Moore.

Ned, Martin and Eddie returned to Dingle and are buried there, while Mossie and Paddy are interred at Killybegs.

On my way home that evening, I reflected on the craic I had with Pat and his boys, Jason and Stevie. Mind you, I didn't establish why Pat's father Martin came all the way up the coast from Kerry to fish out of Killybegs in the first place. In later years, it became almost fashionable for southern fishermen to put down roots in Killybegs, but not so in the early 1930s.

12

WOULDN'T CHANGE A THING

Michael O'Driscoll of Schull, County Cork

It was on a fine August Saturday afternoon that I dropped in on Michael O'Driscoll at his home in the south-west coastal resort and fishing port of Schull, County Cork. We chatted on a patio bathed in sunshine, overlooking the serenity of Schull's picturesque harbour. Michael kept a keen eye on yachts returning from a day race around the Fastnet. He had a special interest in the race outcome as his wife, Eleanor, was crewing on one of the boats.

As with so many others I meet up with these days, Michael comes from a younger generation than myself. I knew his father and mother long before Michael arrived on the scene. His father, Johnny, affectionately known as 'Johnny the *Ros Maolan*' (*Ros Maolan* being the name of a boat he owned and skippered) was a high-profile fisherman associated with the big south-coast fishing boats of the 1950s.

Michael O'Driscoll with Schull Harbour in the background.

From a very early age, it seemed likely that Michael would follow in his father's footsteps and become a fisherman:

My earliest recollections are of being on boats. As a child I used to go out with my father in the summer. I was mad for fishing. He had a boat called the *Linnet* that time. She was a fine beamy boat, fitted with a 95hp Gardner and well suited for seining. As the years passed, trawling was 'coming in big time' and the need for a boat with a more powerful engine arose. In partnership with local man Jimmy O'Reilly and my Uncle Terence [Terence O'Regan], my father purchased the *Sea Wave*. The new owners replaced the original engine with a 230hp Gardner. She was a great boat to tow and remained in the family for seventeen years.

Having succeeded in convincing his mother (not an easy thing to do) that school-based education was not for him, at the age of

15, Michael joined the *Sea Wave* crew on 17 June 1972 – that, he said, 'was my first official day fishing'. He recalls that his father was 'skipper and that the crew were all local and grand men. It was like joining a family, they were all minding me. In the summer time we used a three-bridled trawl to fish for mackerel west of the Mizen and often landed 200 boxes a day.' During the winter it was a case of moving east to fish herring off Cork Harbour, Ballycotton and the Waterford coast. Landing mainly took place at Cobh, with an occasional trip into Dunmore East. An inspection of the *Sea Wave*'s underside in 1976 revealed that she required extensive keel repair work – work that would cost in the region of £40,000! For an ageing boat, that level of expenditure could not be justified and so she was sold on at engine value.

From the early 1970s onwards, it became clear that in order to maximise lucrative herring catches, bigger boats were required. Michael recalled that boats of 70ft and over became the order of the day, and described the arrival of the brand new 75ft Norwegian-built vessels *Marina* and *Cisemair*, owned respectively by Castletownbere men Donal O'Driscoll and Joe-Joe O'Sullivan. There were, he said, 'beautiful and huge boats at the time'. Rolling off BIM yard slipways also were very fine 70ft vessels.

With the *Sea Wave* sold, Michael joined the crew of the 70ft *Breda Helen*, a boat owned and skippered by fellow Schull man John Norris. During the four years that followed, Michael fished on the *Breda Helen* and described John as 'a fine man to fish with'. By then Michael, who was still only 23 years of age, was ready to get his own boat. The phasing-out of boatyards was beginning to kick in and, as a result, having a new boat built had become more difficult:

> My young age didn't help either, and it took the backing of my father to persuade the powers that be to let me have a boat. The arrangement was that should I not be able to make a go of things, then he would step in and take over. At the time,

only Malahide Boatyard showed an interest in building a boat. Representatives of the yard came to Schull armed with plans of a 17m X 5.91m X 2.71m boat, which was I happy to proceed with. Tim Leonard, a fantastic shipwright, was foreman at the yard and oversaw the building of the *Ocean Breeze*, a first-class boat in every way. Launched in 1981, she was powered by a 280hp Kelvin engine. With a transom stern, she carried the beam all the way back. She was an excellent boat to tow.

When I began fishing the *Ocean Breeze*, the crew were my father and my four brothers – a family affair. That's the way it stayed for a number of years until my father became ill and retired. One by one, my brothers went on to do other things, except for one, Terence, who fished with me for twenty years. While other commitments such as having a house built added to the financial burden in the early days, we got by, and it all worked out fine through time.

Michael often made references to his love of pelagic fishing as he spoke. His eyes lit up when he reflected on herring seasons at Dunmore East. It was all pair-fishing by the time he went there with the *Ocean Breeze*:

I was mad for pelagic fishing. I loved the herrings. I don't know if it was because you could catch them so fast, or maybe it was the bit of skill involved. Whitefish trawling I tolerated because there were times when I had no choice. To facilitate pelagic pair-fishing I had the *Ocean Breeze* re-engined in 1991. With nets used getting bigger, my boat lacked the necessary power for pair-fishing. The 280hp Kelvin was replaced by a Cummins 425hp. I believe it was the best move I ever made where the boat was concerned. It greatly enhanced her capabilities. With a 6:1 reduction gear she could tow like hell for her size. She was also very fast – she could do almost 11 knots. While the addition of a shelter deck made her more secure and safer to work on, hindsight suggests that maybe I should have gone for

a bigger boat at the time. Yet, we were doing well and I suppose I settled for the comfortable family lifestyle I had become
accustomed to.

Of the early years' herring fishing out of Dunmore East with
the *Ocean Breeze*, he said:

> I learnt a lot from watching how other skippers went about
> their business. Donal O'Driscoll [of Castletownbere] was a
> fisherman I greatly admired. By observing, bit by bit, I got the
> hang of how things were best done. With fine boats and the
> best of gear, there were a number of very decent and support-
> ive men fishing out of Dunmore. I recall that Dan Leonard and
> his son Brendan were extremely helpful when I was down east;
> couldn't do enough for you and always there when needed.
>
> Throughout the 1990s, I pair-fished with a number of dif-
> ferent boats including, *Francis Maria* (Paul Deasy, Union Hall),
> *Incentive* (Billy Burrell, Duncormick, County Wexford), *Nicola
> Sharon* (Frank Magee, Kilmore Quay), but my long-term part-
> ner was *Breda Helen* under the stewardship of John Norris.
> We worked very successfully for a number of years until John
> retired from fishing. I once landed forty-four tons of herring at
> Dunmore – over 200 cran. The fish were caught about 3 miles
> west of Dunmore on a very calm morning. Frank Magee was
> the last man I pair fished with. As with all good things an end
> finally came along. So it was with the herring fishing of that
> era. Well-documented restrictions and directives from our
> leaders slowly but surely led towards the ending of a splendid
> type of fishing.

Problems conspired to make life very difficult. Initially a chal-
lenging situation arose because Dunmore East Pier didn't have
a weighbridge. That situation gave the powers that be reason
to forbid boats from landing there. That in turn meant the
closest landing facility was at Cobh:

Ocean Breeze (D96) as built in 1991.

Ocean Breeze with shelter deck fitted.

It was very hard those years. We fished a lot in Baginbun Bay, County Wexford, and because of a lack of a weighbridge at Dunmore we had to steam all the way to Cobh [approximately 60 miles]. It was no fun in a 55ft boat loaded with herring. Luckily the weather, for the most part, was good enough with a lot of north and north-west wind, which allowed us to come up along the coast fairly comfortably. Yet, it was a dangerous carry-on! Why a weighbridge was needed for our landings is something that I'll never understand. All our fish was in bins, each weighing 800kg; it was only necessary to count the number of receptacles. For some crazy reason, that wasn't good enough. Instead we were put through the ringer by having to make our way to Cobh, where often we had to wait around for a considerable time until the way was clear to land our catch. Then it was a case of preparing to turn around and steam all the way back to the fishing grounds. I recall one bad night off Tramore while fishing with Frank Magee when I had about 200 cran of herring in a net hanging to the boat. The weather was deteriorating and a passage to Cobh with that load was out of the question. I phoned the department, explained our situation, and asked if we could land at Dunmore. The reply came, short and sweet; we could land a maximum of 50 cran. The rest of the catch we simply had to let go. It was a disgrace and an incident I'll always remember. It occurred at a time when there had been very little fishing because of bad weather. When the one opportunity of making a week's wages came our way it was denied to us because of some incomprehensible ruling.

Gradually, the imposition of restrictions and the closing-down of herring fisheries left me disillusioned. It was also true that fishing around home was not what it used to be. Between one thing and another, I decided to put the boat on the market at a predetermined asking price, which included the licence. Having turned down an offer for the licence only from Galway man Stephen Joyce, he later returned and purchased boat and licence. He transferred the tonnage to his bigger boat and sold the *Ocean Breeze* on to its present owner, Ciaran Powell, Inis Mor [Aran Islands].

Michael's fishing career was not yet over, but this time he looked towards a smaller boat with a view to doing a little trawling locally. He settled on a shelter-decked Cygnus 33, fitted with a 125hp Gardner, which he describes as a lovely boat. He trawled with her for about three years, often on his own, until the onset of arthritis put a stop to that. A period of rest and special medication has largely sorted the problem, though he still has some shoulder discomfort. Despite everything, his love of boats remains unquenched, and with trawling really no longer an option, he has sold the Cygnus and replaced her with a 33ft, twelve-berth angling boat named *Blue Thunder*. During the summer, Michael now likes nothing better than taking parties out on day trips. While many are experienced sea anglers, some don't quite understand that you can't always fish to order. Jokingly, he says, 'some clients seem to believe they are fishing in a kind of supermarket. When they catch a particular species of fish they want to move on and catch a different species. It's like now that we've caught a mackerel lets go and get a few cod.'

The brilliance of reflected sun from the sparkling, gentle waves of scenic Schull Harbour was still much in evidence as the afternoon wore on. Our conversation drifted on to topics removed from Michael's fishing career. He spoke of his mother, Alice, a native of Sherkin Island, then in her eighty-sixth year and still going strong – she'd pass for 70 – up every morning at 7 a.m., out to Mass, baking and playing cards during the winter. He went on to say, 'She's amazing, mentally superb and was boss of the family for as long as I can remember. You'll never see women like her again.' I too have memories of Alice as a glamorous young lady arriving in Baltimore off the Sherkin ferry. She must then have been in her late teens or early twenties. When I met her in more recent years and mistook her for her sister Eileen, who I also remember as a glamorous young lady with a wonderful singing voice, she told me in no uncertain terms that she was *not* Eileen.

Now happy and contented with a family lifestyle that includes pampering a number of precious grandchildren, Michael's parting words were, 'I wouldn't change a thing in my life if I had to do it all over again.'

13

THROW HIM OUT!

John Francis Brosnan of Dingle, County Kerry

At long last I got back to Dingle. My visit was well overdue. A number of years ago, when sourcing information for my book *Sea Change* (about BIM 50-footers), John Francis very kindly loaned me photographs and other printed materials. In fact, one of the photos, that of the *Ros Arcan*, was chosen for the front cover of the book. It was an excellent choice. Many thanks to the patient gentleman who never once contacted me regarding the return of his cherished possessions. All are now safely back with their owner. At his Cooleen home, we sat and talked about one thing and another, not least his current period of convalescence following back surgery. As a man steeped in the commercial fishing tradition, it wasn't long until we got around to discussing his personal experiences.

John Francis comes from long-established west Kerry fishing stock, with his father and grandfather having sailed from Dingle to harvest fish in local waters. Memories of his father Thomas includes being aware that he owned a Killybegs-built boat named *Rory*. Although John Francis wasn't born until 1947, as he grew up, he was told of the hardships endured by boat owners and fishermen during the late 1930s and early '40s. 'There wasn't much money in fishing then,' he said. However, in the years immediately following the Second World War, things improved greatly; prices and demand for mackerel were at a premium. With a smile on his face, he said, 'My father always told me that 1947, the year I was born, was a great year all round.' He recalled too that his father was a man of great faith, who knelt to pray at a kitchen chair each morning before heading off on a day's fishing.

Thomas Brosnan, known locally as 'Tommy Blocks' because of his physical build, parted company with the *Rory* in 1954 and replaced her with the Baltimore-built BIM 50-footer *Ros Brin*. John Francis was then 7 years of

John Francis Brosnan relaxing at his Dingle home.

age. In 1962, following a prolonged illness, his father died at the age of 53. It was a devastating blow for his wife and young family. While his father was still in hospital, family circumstances required John Francis to leave school at the age of 14 and take up employment as a fisherman. He joined the crew of the late Brendan O'Flaherty's *Ros Mult*. During the two years John Francis fished with Brendan, whom he describes as, 'of the old school and a great fisherman', they concentrated on lobster-fishing and trawling. In the summer months they worked along the west coast on the lobster trail, while in wintertime they went in search of flat fish in Dingle Bay. It was, 'a brilliant time: summer was summer and winter was winter. You could go off for a whole week during the summer and be sure of fine weather. There was a pile of fish to be caught then. With 120 barrel pots you could get four or five dozen lobsters a day. There were also massive fish. While most of the Dingle 50-footers of that era were "ringers", Brendan stuck to trawling.'

When the time came for John Francis to move on, he joined the crew of Paddy Flannery's BIM 56-footer, *Guiding Star*. He recalls trawling off the Clare coast and up as far as Galway:

Then there was, of course, the herring fishing at Dunmore East, and also Killybegs, where we spent one season. The Dunmore fishing was big time. At first we worked on our own using a three-bridled net. Later we went pairing with the *Ard Fionnbarr*, a boat then owned by Paddy Flannery's brother, Michael. It was great. We got loads of fish, occasionally filled to the top of the hold, maybe 130 cran. There was a few bob to be made then. It came in very handy. Eileen and I married in 1972. We were starting a family and so on. The years of the 1970s and early '80s were great years in all aspects of fishing, whether at sea or ashore. Anyone interested could walk down the pier and get a job.

He went on to say:

> The banning of salmon drift netting is very sad because it has killed off fishing in many small ports around the coast – communities and families depended on it, and encouraged teenagers to take up fishing. Take tourism out of Dingle now and you could close the door; fishing is gone.

Interestingly, John Francis mentioned that Spanish trawlers, like our own, are now mostly manned by non-nationals, and went on to say, 'The old style of Spanish fishing and crews hailing from home ports is practically gone. Now many crew members are natives of South America.'

Following his years on Paddy Flannery's *Guiding Star*, John Francis and his brother Timmy Joe fished the *Fiona Patricia*, a boat owned by local man, Jimmy Fenton. They engaged in trawling until Castletownbere man, Larry Murphy, a great fisherman, came on the scene. With Larry as skipper, John Francis, his brothers Timmy Joe and Thomas, his nephew Pat 'Bawn' (son of the famous Kerry Gaelic footballer Paddy 'Brawn' Brosnan), another Castletownbere man, and Brendan Cahalane from west of Dingle, made up the crew of the *Fiona Patricia*. Herring pair-fishing was by then (the 1970s) well established. Under Larry's guidance, the *Fiona Patricia* and the *Kenure*, owned and skippered by Skerries man, Tom Ferguson, formed a highly successful partnership. John Francis recalls, 'The bigger boats were able to carry more fish and the price of herring was steadily rising.'

Mention of the *Fiona Patricia/Kenure* partnership reminded me of a story Tom Ferguson told me. It appears that on a particular day at Dunmore East, while landings were generally low, their boats hit the jackpot with full loads of fish for which top prices were paid. It was, Tom said, 'one of our greatest landings. On the same day over the phone my wife Dolores asked me to suggest a name for our newly born daughter.

The *Ros Airgead* – former pride of the BIM 50-footers – lies as a derelict wreck near Dingle.

I had no hesitation in suggesting Fiona, so pleased was I with the *Fiona Patricia/Kenure* lucrative catch. The baby was indeed named Fiona.'

Around late 1980s, maybe into the 1990s, in partnership with a local businessman, John Francis became involved with the 40m MFV *Drakkar*. He fished her for a year and a half or so, trawling as far away as the Porcupine Banks. It was a time when crews were becoming difficult to get. In those years, he also became involved with another boat, the 66ft Scotch-built *Altair*. 'I went on her myself and got a skipper for the *Drakkar*. The *Drakkar* was built in France in 1957. As such, she was not a young boat when she came to Dingle and as the years passed she began to deteriorate. When the time came to end her days, having been sold for scrap, she was cut up in Spain.'

The story of the *Altair* was very different. Her lifetime was unexpectedly cut short. While fishing off the Blasket Islands about a year after her arrival in Dingle, an engine room explosion caused a fire, which resulted in the boat becoming a write-off:

> There were four of us fishing on her – myself, my son Garry and two other men. Out of the blue, we heard this terrifying explosion – a fierce explosion below in the engine room and up she went in a blaze. Clouds of black smoke, accompanied by horrific acrid fumes, belched up from below deck. There was nothing I could do, I didn't even have time to send out a mayday message. Within seconds, or so it seemed, the thick black fumes became unbearable. All electronics were wiped out by the explosion. I stumbled out of the wheelhouse and set about getting the lads off the boat as quickly as possible. We were in the life raft within a matter of minutes. Via mobile phone, I made contact with another trawler and asked its skipper to send out a mayday. The lifeboat quickly arrived on the scene and some of her crew boarded the *Altair* in an attempt to extinguish the fire. With no hope of getting down to the engine room, they decided to break a hole in the deck. Easier said than done; the deck proved extremely resistant to breakage. Eventually the fire was brought under control. By now the other trawler had appeared on the scene and, with the fire extinguished, we went back on board in order to save our fishing gear. We transferred the wires over to our colleagues in the other boat and they hauled it for us. The lifeboat towed the *Altair* to Dingle. Exploding batteries were deemed responsible for the high drama experienced and indeed for the terrifying ordeal suffered by the crew. The *Altair* was not to fish again.

Though not as daunting as the explosion experience on the *Altair*, John Francis had yet another scary sea tale to tell. The background to it is that he and his brother Timmy Joe (possibly along with some others) went to Killybegs to bring the recently purchased boat home to Dingle. As they were about to set off on the southwards trip, for whatever reason, an engineer who was to accompany them decided against it. John Francis and Timmy Joe headed off anyway. Weather conditions were not good initially and worsened as they came down along the coast. They first experienced concern when elements of the boat's electronics gradually began to fail. More worrying was the realisation that the boat's compass was reading inaccurately. After two days at sea, they had no idea where they were. They reckoned afterwards that, having come south a good part of the way, they somehow went back north, before again heading south. Eventually, the sighting of a coaster led to them to discovering their location. Having fired some flares to attract the attention of the coaster's crew, in poor weather conditions the coaster came close enough communicate. The 'lost souls' were to learn that they were currently off Loop Head, County Clare. The skipper of the coaster confirmed he was going south and planned on passing through the Blasket Sound. The invitation to tag along was gratefully received by the Brosnan brothers. The eventual sight of the Blaskets was one of pure joy for the Dingle men. As John Francis said, 'Once in sight of the Blaskets we knew our own coastline.' It was only when they got a chance to look around the boat they realised what a mess she was in. 'There was,' he said, 'water everywhere. The weather had been so bad that seas coming in over the boat kept washing bits of gear and other items back along the deck. I can tell you, we were glad to see Dingle on Sunday morning.'

When I asked if there was anything besides fishing that he remembered about Dingle from his young days, he immediately mentioned the train; even though he was only 6 years of age in 1953 when it stopped running, he remembers it going right to the top of the pier. I'm not sure if he remembers, or if he was told, but apparently his relations, women in particular, used to send a lot of fish to the Dublin market on the train. He also remembered the last day the train ran, when he

Timmy Joe Brosnan.

and several other children were loaded onto a wagon or van of sorts and taken for a run out to Lispole and back.

All good things come to an end and so it was with my visit to the genial John Francis. About to leave, tongue in cheek, I mentioned to my host that there was something he had forgotten to tell me about. He laughed heartily and said:

> I know what you are on about, and yes, it did happen. I was a 19-year-old at the time and a crew member on Joe Walsh's 56-footer *Morning Star*. We came to the pier one evening, after a day's fishing, with a sturgeon lying on the deck. We had been trying to keep it alive all day. A crowd had gathered, including a film crew. There was obviously great interest in the fish. Someone shouted, 'Throw him out', meaning throw the fish on to the pier. I misunderstood and threw him overboard! The aghast reaction of the crowd immediately alerted me to the

fact that I had done something wrong. Glancing up, I saw what looked like a hundred people staring at me. It was the most embarrassing thing ever. As a further consequence I didn't register high on Joe Walsh's most liked person of the week.

14

REFLECTIONS OF AN OCTOGENARIAN

Frank Kiernan of Kinsale, County Cork

On bright summer mornings in the 1950s, while still in my late teens, I recall driving a van from Union Hall to Kinsale Pier, where I collected fish for the Cork markets. In stark contrast to today's bustling fashionable resort, Kinsale was then a drab and uninspiring place that abounded with disused semi-derelict buildings. For the most part, the only seagoing craft in sight were a few fishing boats tied up at the pier. How that scenario has changed! Today, the norm is to a town centre chock-a-block with traffic, a profusion of seafront maritime activities, footpaths heaving with people, and parking spaces at an absolute premium. Thankfully, on a more recent visit to the town, I didn't have to look for a parking space because, Frank Kiernan, the gentleman I had arranged to meet up with, had reserved a spot for me at the Pier Head (Customs Quay).

By reputation, I knew of Frank to be deeply engrossed in maritime matters, particularly those related to the furtherance of Kinsale as a shipping seaport. At the time of our meeting, he was in his early eighties, yet he showed no visible signs of his age. Indeed, he had the comportment of an active 65-year-old. Inviting me for coffee, he skipped across the road to the Yacht Club with me trailing behind.

Described as a main company contact by the Institute of Chartered Shipbrokers, he was at that time associated with Waterlands Shipping & Warehousing Ltd at Kinsale port. Frank had retired many years previously but had been enticed back in an advisory capacity by his former employers.

Comfortably seated in the Yacht Club, he opened our chat by relating early memories of large fleets of Arklow boats coming to Kinsale drift netting. 'They came,' he said, 'mackerel-fishing in springtime and herring-fishing in winter.' The names of visiting boats rolled off his tongue – *St Veronica*, *Hidden Treasure*, *Evelyn*, *Avonbeg* and many others. 'Those,' he said, 'are just a few that come to mind. Each boat had a crew of six or seven men. The shopkeepers were delighted with them. The skippers and owners had a great reputation for paying their bills.' He went on to say, 'Kinsale, as with all ports, had its ups and downs. There was very big fishing here in the mid-1920s and a lot of money was made. Then came the collapse; things got very bad, it was a serious setback for the town.' As an afterthought he lightheartedly recalled his aspirations to become a fisherman:

I went out one night mackerel-drifting in the Dixon family-owned *St Veronica* [Arklow]. It was one of the worst experiences of my life! I was down in the cabin, which had this enormous boiler situated at one end. The heat it emitted was unbearable. I was so sick. The excessive heat, the noise, the rolling and tossing of the boat all conspired to over-whelm. That finished me with fishing. I don't know what the crew of the *Veronica* told my father; obviously it was their idea of a joke, but he came along and said to me, Frank, the crew of *Veronica* were very impressed with you, there's a berth for you anytime you want it. I said nothing but my mind was well and truly made up – no berth for me, thank you very much.

Frank's father, Frank (Snr), was a fish buyer who acted as an agent for a number of main merchants over the years. He began his career in the early 1900s as a buyer for a prominent Liverpool-based firm whose proprietor was one Hugo Flynn. The job took him to ports such as Baltimore, Dunmore East and Howth. All was going well until the advent of Irish independence. It was a development that did not rest easily with the Flynn-owned organisation, as was the case with many English-based firms and companies of that era. As the saying goes, they pulled the plug. All operations in Ireland were terminated. Flynn's had also been big-time turkey buyers. The departure of such firms from our shores had a seriously detrimental impact on employment.

Kinsale Harbour.

Always close to activities that went on around the pier, Frank has fond memories of the Heir Island lobster-fishing men who came to Kinsale in his young days. 'They were,' he said, 'lovely men. I once went with them on a trip to Cobh to collect bait.' He explained that the bait was sent by fish merchants, Clayton Love & Sons, from Cork, to Cobh by train, where, weather permitting, the Heir Island men collected it on Sundays. This is how he remembers the trip:

Off we went on a lovely morning in a boat powered by one of the famous 13/15hp Kelvin engines. It was great: we had mugs of tea, bastable bread, jam and everything; living like lords. We arrived in Cobh, collected the bait and heading back from the station carrying the boxes by the hoop-iron bands fitted on each end, we made our towards the boat. They were as happy as Larry, swinging the boxes as they walked along. Then the word went out: they should have '*one*' before they left for Kinsale. All agreed and up we went to this pub called the Seagull. I can assure you there was a lot more than '*one*'! I know I had Little Norah [a brand name] lemonade coming out of my ears! Then the singing started. There were lovely singers amongst them. The songs sung that day later became very popular in traditional Irish music circles. Eventually they decided it was time to head off back to Kinsale. Going down the harbour all was fine but when we turned west the boat started jumping all over the place. The weather had changed greatly since morning. The Little Norah's and I soon parted company, with one of the men holding me by the ass of the trousers as I hung out over the side of the boat. That night I decided that I would definitely never go out in a boat again. In fact, apart from the occasional annual yachting trip, that proved to be the case.

The time came for Frank to begin thinking of a career. Reports from school were not at all encouraging – the 'Brothers' (religious order teachers) were unimpressed by his application and progress. This led to his father becoming proactive and, without informing the so-labelled 'reluctant student', lined him up with a job – an assistant at a hardware store:

> To make matters worse, my father introduced me to my new employer as a fellow who wanted to become a hardware merchant. I didn't know what he was talking about. It got even more distressing when told I would be required to wear a brown store coat. To add insult to injury, my first task was to sweep the floor. When the boss saw how I was going about it, with a sigh of exasperation, he said, 'You were told to sprinkle *a little* water to keep the dust down, not flood the shop!' I was not at all happy doing such a menial job. How degrading is this, I thought? What will the lads say when they see me sweeping floors and wearing a brown coat!

Nevertheless, Frank stayed on for seven years, at the end of which, he said, 'Clearly I wasn't getting anywhere. However, by then I was a fairly mature kind of individual.'

The possibility of a new avenue leading to employment more in keeping with Frank's leanings came along when owners of a French fish-canning factory, with a parent factory at Concarneau, Brittany, decided to set up a similar business at Kinsale. At a job interview, Frank made the most of his father's involvement with the fishing industry. Perhaps that swung things in his favour. At any rate, he was successful. Initially he was posted to the Concarneau factory for the purpose of familiarising himself with the processes involved. On the factory floor and under the wing of the company's industrial chemist, he quickly learnt the ropes. The procedure was slick enough. Not surprisingly, great emphasis was placed on maximising returns from fish processed. A minimum number of cans for a given quantity of fish was an essential requirement. With that, and other aspects of the factory-floor operation clearly understood, Frank returned home and took on responsibility for overseeing the smooth running of output at the newly built factory, known as 'Kinsale Canners'. With a highly respected and permanently Kinsale-based Frenchman manager, all went well from the beginning (around the mid-1950s).

A variety of fish species were processed and canned, with a large part of the output being exported to French West African countries. There were around forty women and eight or nine men employed. It should be said that they worked long hours and in conditions that would be unlikely to meet today's stringent health and safety requirements. Nevertheless, as Frank put it, 'We were six-and-a-half years running and going grand. Then, unexpectedly, things came to a halt! Bad news was broken to us by the manager.' He stunned Frank and other senior personnel with the announcement, 'I believe in the long term we are finished here.'

The factory did indeed close down. It came about as a circuitous consequence of independence being granted to some French West African countries. So ended a business enterprise that had brought a glimpse of light and activity to an otherwise rock-bottom mid-1950s Kinsale.

In the 1960s, Frank became involved in some of Kinsale's public bodies. While the closure of the canning factory was a setback, he believes that its being there gave the industrial side of the town an impetus that had previously been absent. He quotes examples of an American clothing manufacturer and a German perforated steel factory coming to the area in the years that followed. 'Things began to pick up,' he said. The arrival of yet another American company in 1981 was later to have a significant influence on Frank's future way of life. The company Eli Lilly, manufacturers of active ingredients for a number of important medicines, were planning to set up a plant at Dunderrow, 7 or 8 miles from Kinsale. Central to the project going ahead was the installation of an outfall pipe leading from the factory to the little bay of Sandycove, located

just five minutes' drive from Kinsale. Guarantees were given
that, as Frank put it, 'there would be nothing damaging in the
way of pollution or otherwise as a result of the outfall.' Yet,
not surprisingly, the proposed development became very con-
troversial locally. Frank, who was then an established member
of Kinsale Harbour Commissioners, for which he served as
chairman in 1978 and 1981, was in favour of the project on
the basis that the setting up of a prestigious factory hinged
on it. He foresaw that Eli Lilly had the potential to become
a big local employer and that hindering its establishment was
playing fast and loose with people's livelihoods. While there
was a difference of opinion among Harbour Board members,
a majority voted to give the project their backing. The backing was a significant contributing factor in Eli Lilly getting
the go-ahead. Recognising it as such, the factory managing
director attended a Harbour Board meeting to thank all concerned for their support. As a gesture, the company donated a
Chain of Office to Kinsale Harbour Board – an insignia that
had not previously existed. Additionally, the managing direc-
tor asked if there was anything else the company could do to
help the board. Frank, not one to miss an opportunity, stood
up and explained that there was great local interest in reviving
shipping at Kinsale but that there was a problem because of
silting-up at the quay. When asked how Eli Lilly could help
with that problem, Frank outlined his thoughts on the matter
as follows: 'The company has a vessel ploughing a trench for
the outfall pipe at Sandycove and if the Harbour Board had
its services for a couple of hours I'm sure it would solve our
problem at the quay.' The managing director took the sug-
gestion to the factory owners, who responded positively.
Discussions took place between the Harbour Board engineer
and experts associated with the vessel, which resulted in the
sea area adjacent to the quay being made suitable for ships
to come alongside. A great step forward had been achieved
where shipping possibilities at the port were concerned.

The next step was to get importers interested in using Kinsale as a shipping port. That aspiration soon came to fruition. Waterlands Shipping & Warehousing Ltd took the initiative with a 600-ton coaster making grain landings for R&D Hall, Ireland's biggest importer and supplier of animal feed. With Frank having been appointed to co-ordinate ship arrivals, departures and all aspects of stevedoring, the port quickly developed to a point where it handled around sixty vessels per year. The largest single cargo, 4,300 tons of maize, was landed by the Arklow Shipping vessel *Arklow Rival* for Irish distillers, Middleton, a company that imports around 65,000 tons of grain per year. I asked Frank what his exact title was within the was in the business. He laughed and said, 'I'm the after-hours man who is contacted by ships' captains as they approach the coast. It could be on any day of the year, and at any hour of day or night. I arrange for a pilot to go out. I then contact all concerned with unloading the vessel to ensure that the show is on the road by 7 a.m.'

All appeared to be going well at Kinsale port. Then, out of the blue, on 27 March 2013, they received notice of the closure of the company's Kinsale operation, effective from 29 July 2013. Job losses and loss of port revenue was an inevitable consequence. Frank said, 'I put my heart and soul into Waterlands, loved it, enjoyed the success and made wonderful contacts and friends.' He is nevertheless optimistic of a revival, 'as there are a few reputable companies interested in doing business at the port'. Let's hope that will be the case.

So, how is it that an octogenarian was still actively employed? 'Well,' Frank said, 'I retired fifteen years ago and basically the company couldn't get anybody else to do a job with such erratic and unsociable hours, so they asked if I would consider helping out. I jumped at it. I was delighted! I've always been well looked after by the company and I found it of great interest to be down on the quay, meeting and talking to people. It was great psychologically.' Should normal port activities return, would he be interesting in going back to work? Without hesitation, he replies, 'Yes, I'd be delighted.'

In 2012, when Cork County Council took over administration duties from Kinsale Harbour Board, Frank had been a Harbour Commissioner for forty-seven consecutive years. It's no small wonder that, following the takeover, Simon Coveney, TD, then Minister for Agriculture, Food and the Marine, forwarded a congratulatory letter to the man who had given unstintingly of his time over so many years. Noteworthy too were the reported special tributes paid to Frank at a winding-up meeting of the board.

A final item of interest recalled by Frank was that his mother, as a young girl, was on telephone switchboard duties at Kinsale post office on 7 May 1915 when over the airwaves came a communiqué to the effect that the Cunard liner *Lusitania* was sinking 11 miles off the Old Head of Kinsale. As the saying goes, 'all hell broke loose'. To cope with the volumes of messages being relayed, six telephone appliances, along with operators, were promptly dispatched from Cork to Kinsale. Soon it became clear that the loss of lives was huge. The final fatality figure of 1,198 was met with worldwide disbelief.

A great afternoon was had in Frank's company – both interesting and entertaining. May his zest for life and longevity continue long into the future.

ACKNOWLEDGEMENTS

As in my previous book, *Following the Shoals*, it is to the memories of the seagoing men of Ireland that I have turned my attention. To those I chatted with, I extend my sincere thanks for the interest shown in my research, the time taken to relate their stories, the hospitality shown, the humour and the encouraging remarks that came my way. On the topic of hospitality, it would be amiss not to mention the sustenance provided by the good ladies encountered along the way.

As the images were such an integral part of the book, I offer my sincere thanks to all who contributed in that respect.

I, too, greatly acknowledge the unstinting encouragement, help and tolerance from my wife, Una, my son and daughters.

When alighting from buses in certain parts of the country, I've noted that young females frequently thank the driver with the words, 'Thanks a million'. Somehow I feel the expression gives an extra dimension to the more familiar words of gratitude usually expressed. As such, to all those people who in anyway helped in furthering my dream of writing this book, I say, 'Thanks a million'.